THE CURRY CLUB INDIAN RESTAURANT COOKBOOK

THE CURRY CLUB INDIAN RESTAURANT COOKBOOK

Pat Chapman

PIATKUS

© 1984 Pat Chapman
First published in 1984
by Judy Piatkus (Publishers) Limited of London
Reprinted 1984

British Library Cataloguing in Publication Data
Chapman, Pat
  The Curry Club Indian restaurant cookbook.
  1. Cookery, India
  I. Title
  641.5954   TX724.5.I4

  ISBN 0-86188-488-4

Edited by Susan Fleming
Designed by Susan Ryall
Illustrated by Hanife Hassan

Phototypeset by Tradespools Limited, Frome, Somerset
Printed in Great Britain by Butler & Tanner Ltd, Frome and London

CONTENTS

MEASURES

Measurements are very precise indeed when written down. The trouble is that we are stuck between Imperial and metric measures, and then spoon sizes also vary between countries.

My advice is to read for interest only and then use for rough guidance only. In practice you probably own several teaspoons which are all different sizes and in any case who has the equipment to measure 5 grammes accurately?

Throughout the recipes I use teaspoon, dessertspoon (about 2 teaspoons), and tablespoon measures. Treat these as guides. If you like the taste of one spice, for example, in preference to another, put a bit more of that in. An American tablespoon holds 14.2 ml and is slightly smaller than the Imperial tablespoon which holds 17.3 ml, and the large metric spoon which holds 15 ml. The Australian tablespoon holds 20 ml. But, as you can appreciate, the differences are quite minimal, and don't matter a jot!

I also use cup measures – which is handy for liquids (although I occasionally measure some solids by cup as well). In each case these cups are a tea cup or wine glass, which hold 6 fluid ounces or 175 ml.

As to the oven temperatures quoted below, these too are a guide. The temperature an oven actually cooks at can vary enormously from what the dial says, especially on the cheaper ones. You'll know your own oven, so simply use your common sense.

The true skill in any cooking is to learn to be flexible. Then you become innovative and your cooking becomes an art.

Oven Temperatures	°F	°C	Gas
Very cool	225	110	¼
Very slow	250	120	½
Slow or cool	275	140	1
Very moderate	300	150	2
Moderate	325	160	3
	350	180	4
Moderately hot	375	190	5
	400	200	6
Hot	425	220	7
	450	230	8
Very hot	475	240	9

INTRODUCTION

There are dozens of Indian cookery books available on the market. Many include unobtainable ingredients, baffling techniques and pages of description. I have yards of these books on my shelf. Reading them is a great adventure: 'Roast this or that mystery spice for 1.75 minutes, grind it to ½ mm pieces, fry for 17 seconds in jumping-bean fat at 316°F then add it to another mystery spice. Soak in hokum-cokum water for 2 days then blanch in the midday sun at 81°F.' The recipe rambles on and on, culminating with a warning that if you depart from this or that age-old technique the flavour will be ruined. The recipes have probably been in the writers' families for generations, and no doubt produce fine dishes. You may even enjoy the challenge.

At the other extreme is the dreaded curry powder. Whenever you see a recipe or a cookbook that exhorts you to add curry powder, ignore it. The curry you cook may turn out well, but you will be unable to vary the flavours from dish to dish and recipe to recipe.

The road to delicious curries, authentic or restaurant flavour, home-cooked yet professional in appearance, is somewhere in between these two options. Providing you can tell the time and are prepared to experiment and practise, you will be able to produce snacks, meals or banquets that will enable you to ignore your local takeaway from now on, and will leave most Indian restaurants at the starting gate.

Try a recipe which takes your fancy first. The instructions are straightforward, the ingredients easily obtainable, and the spices, which are usually the stumbling block, are listed clearly and separately (in fact many are available, ready ground etc, from The Curry Club and are marked SP *Spice pack available*). The result should be a super dish which you'll want to make again. Next time you may want to make a few changes to suit you. Don't be afraid to experiment. The wonder of Indian cookery is its flexibility. In many dishes you can leave spices out, put extra in, cook longer or shorter, cook hotter or cooler, in an oven casserole, or on top of the stove, obtain a thicker or thinner texture. You can freeze many, prepare them a day or two before or serve straightaway. Each variation may result in a change of taste or texture to your dish . . . but it should always be delicious. There are few hard and fast rules to Indian cookery. Like good wines, there is an infinite variety of tastes. The margin for error is enormous – and you can correct most mistakes.

No two Indian cookery books will prepare the same recipe in the same way, neither will any two Indian chefs. It is hardly surprising in a cuisine that goes back many thousands of years and which even now is largely handed down by word of mouth. As you can get used to dealing with spices you may find that you do not need to measure precisely nor time exactly. You'll use your senses – you'll know by touch, taste, sight, smell and even sound whether your dish is cooking correctly, and if not, what to do about it.

This book is a selection of well-tested recipes combining many restaurant favourites with a liberal sprinkling of recipes you'll find in Indian homes. They have all been tested by researchers and members of The Curry Club. Started in 1982, the Club caters for all the needs of people who enjoy curry. Its aim is to impart curry information from recipes to restaurant reports, cookery demonstrations and courses, gourmet curry nights, gourmet trips to India, and a lot more (see Appendix 1).

That Restaurant Flavour

Most of us are introduced to Indian food at the Indian restaurant. But when it comes to capturing the restaurant flavour it seems to elude all the cookery books I've seen.

In fact it's the question I get asked most: 'How do I get the same flavour in my curry as my local Indian restaurant?' The answer, as you might suspect, is very much more complex than the question. Given that your local restaurant does not produce 'unique curries', nor has any 'unique methods' for doing so, and given that your local restaurant produces a 'standard flavour', why is it so different from home-cooking flavours?

Firstly, technique and practice. The chef or cook at the average restaurant will be churning out several hundred dishes every day. He learns quickly and repeatedly to get the texture right. How much practice does the average home curry cook get?

Secondly, a professional must watch his costs, and in this country time is money. So he looks for time-saving ingredients and techniques. He will probably use garlic and ginger powder in place of fiddly skinning, chopping and frying fresh items. He may use dehydrated onion flakes in place of fresh. More than likely he will use a quick method to obtain an onion purée (see page 30). For example, he may boil his onions then electrically purée them, then fry them.

He will more than likely produce a standard curry gravy using basic spices (turmeric, coriander, cummin, paprika, garlic powder, ginger powder, etc) to which he will add taste enhancers – factory-bottled curry paste, garam masala, asafoetida, fenugreek seeds or dry leaves and even some chemicals. Monosodium glutamate enhances taste and thickens sauces. He varies each dish but uses his sauce as his base.

Probably he will achieve the bright oranges, reds, yellows and brown colours using powdered food colouring ... and tinned tomatoes and tomato purée and ketchup, and sweeteners such as sugar or even puréed mango chutney in dishes such as patia. And lastly he cooks in large batches in large pans where the margin of error is enormous, when the odd tablespoonful or two of this or that over or under will not matter. At home, half a *teaspoon* over or under will alter the flavour of a dish for four.

We can use some or all of these techniques if we choose. But we have the opportunity to produce dishes which will equal and better most average restaurants. My aim is to bring you a well-rounded selection of recipes which will enable you to turn out anything from a huge feast to a simple TV supper or snack. You probably won't get around to trying them all (although I hope you do). Give yourself a few trial runs, and be patient if things don't quite work out the first or second time. Before long you'll be inventing your own dishes and entertaining your friends to fare that no restaurant could hope to equal. Then I won't mind if you never read this book again – it will have done its job!

Pat Chapman
The Curry Club
Haslemere   May 1984

1
USEFUL INFORMATION

In this first chapter, I include some basic information which will help you with your larder stores, special fresh ingredients and kitchen equipment. I also give some hints about freezing, about serving and eating Indian food (the whole point of the book, of course), as well as, although of course it won't happen to you, how to rectify any disasters!

In Appendix 2 I have made a complete list of special items which are used throughout the book, dividing them into essential and non-essential ingredients. This should ease any beginner's turmoil!

Spices

At first sight it is the spice department which might put you off the whole idea of Indian cooking. *Dozens* of herbs and spices are used. Some crop up only occasionally, and you can produce a wide range of recipes with a sensible number. But one thing is for sure: *never* buy curry powder. It's a bland factory-produced mixture of the cheaper spices and probably a good helping of sawdust off the factory floor, and it makes all dishes taste the same. No self-respecting Indian cook would consider using curry powder. It is the selective use of spices which makes each Indian dish individual and subtle.

Most spices can be obtained from health-food shops, or the larger supermarkets. If you have Indian shops near you they will stock all the items you'll need. The simplest way to get exactly what you want is by using The Curry Club itself. The Mail Order Department is one of the most useful services The Curry Club offers its members. It has a wide range of spices and herbs, dry foods, teas, cookware, tableware and gift items. And it supplies pre-mixed spices for Curry Club recipes in sensible sized packs. Spices are always freshly roasted, ground and blended and are despatched to you on the same day, stocks permitting. For the current Mail Order list, write to the Club (see Appendix 1).

GRINDING SPICES

It is better by far to grind your own whole spices whenever you can. Firstly you can be sure of the quality and contents, and secondly they will be fresher and tastier. The traditional method is by mortar and pestle, but you can use an electric coffee grinder. After a damp wipe it can still be used for coffee – it might even enhance the flavour! Use small quantities to prevent overloading the motor.

Don't try to grind dry ginger or turmeric. They are far too fibrous for most small grinders, and commercial powders are adequate. Peppers – chilli, paprika and black or white pepper – are tricky, and commercially ground powders will suffice. The oilier spices such as cloves, nutmeg, brown cardamoms and bay leaves are easier to grind if roasted first.

ROASTING SPICES

Whole spices are roasted to enhance or change the flavour. The process is simple and can be done in a dry pan on the stove, in a dry electric frying pan, or in the oven. Each spice should be heated until it gives off an aroma. The heat should be medium rather than hot and the time required is a few minutes. The spice should not blacken, a light brown at most is sufficient. The original oil of the spice must not be totally cooked out or it will lose its flavour. A little experimenting will soon show you how to do it. In some recipes pre-roasted spices are important (see Garam Masala, page 31).

STORING SPICES

Whole spices retain their flavour longer than ground, for one year or more sometimes. Ground spices give off a stronger aroma than whole, and of course this means their storage life is that much shorter. Three months is about right for most ground items. So plan your larder accordingly, and buy little and often and grind freshly. Keep the spices out of sunlight (better in a dark pantry) and in airtight labelled containers. Coffee or jam jars are excellent.

Dry Foods

Rice, lentils, Bombay duck, papadams and flour are all a part of Indian cookery ... some more important than others. They will all store indefinitely.

RICE *(see also Chapter 8)*

If your first introduction to rice was stodgy rice pudding – that particularly English invention – you'd be forgiven for underestimating the importance of rice. It is only with the growth of Chinese and Indian restaurants in this country that the appeal of rice has widened. Throughout Asia, rice is a staple food and is eaten with many curry dishes. There are dozens of types, but you should always use a long-grained rice. The best and most commonly used is Basmati which has a superb flavour and cooks well. You can use Patna rice, or American long-grain, although neither has the same flavour (the American is polished, and this removes some of the taste, texture and protein value). Don't use short-grained or round rice, which will simply not cook into fluffy or separate grains. There are several methods of cooking – steaming, absorption, casseroling and, perhaps the easiest, boiling.

LENTILS *(see also Chapter 8)*

Red split lentils (masoor dhal) are the commonest, but there are dozens of other types. You won't need to stock them all, though, and I suggest just five – masoor, channa, moong green, toor and whole urid (black). Of those only masoor is really essential.

Always pick through lentils to ensure there is no grit etc, and wash well prior to cooking. It is usually best to soak lentils overnight (minimum 6 hours) before you cook them. This softens them and speeds up the cooking process. Rinse the lentils first then put the same quantity of lentils to water into a bowl large enough to allow the lentils to expand to double their dry size.

Lentils can be ground in a coffee grinder where recipes require.

BOMBAY DUCK

Bombay duck is a fish which abounds in the rivers and estuaries around Bombay. There it is known as Bommaloe Macchli or Machi. After it is caught, it is topped, tailed and filleted and then hung on cane frames to dry. We receive it in this dried form and it will keep indefinitely in a screw-top jar out of the sun. It can be used in a curry or pickles (see Bombay Duck Pickle, page 148) or, more commonly, as a crispy salty nibble with an aperitif, or crumbled over your curry and rice as a garnish.

To cook, deep-fry until golden and serve warm. Its strong fishy smell diminishes on cooking, but it is still an acquired taste.

PAPADAMS

These thin 6 inch (15 cm) diameter wafers are made from lentil flour, and make an excellent snack starter to an Indian-style meal. Buy them ready-made – you need continuous hot sun and a lifetime's training to make them yourself! They come plain, or spiced with cummin seeds, chilli, peppercorns, dhal or garlic.

To cook them, preheat the deep-fryer until quite hot. Test heat by dropping a tiny piece of papadam into the fat. It should pop up to the surface at once, not sink. When fat is hot enough, put papadams in, one at a time. They will whiten at once and enlarge a bit (if they don't, fat is not hot enough). Remove when it begins to change shape and colour (about 20 seconds). Shake off excess oil, stand upright for a few minutes, then serve hot – or keep in warming drawer or low oven.

They can also be grilled when, obviously, no fat is needed.

FLOUR

In many parts of the Indian sub-continent wheat is the staple food – not rice. The basic flours used for Indian breads are *wholemeal flour* (the Indian version is called *ata flour* and is available from Asian suppliers or The Curry Club), *self-raising flour* and *strong plain white flour*.

You'll also find the following useful to keep in stock: *gram flour (besan)* which is made from channa dhal (lentils), and is used to make bhajias, pakoras etc (see Chapter 3); *rice flour* which is less important but useful if you need to thicken a gravy and don't want the wheat taste you get from ordinary flour. It is also used to make sweetmeats.

TAMARIND

Tamarind is a very sour date-like fruit, pod-like in shape, which grows on trees all over India. It can be plucked and used fresh, but we know it more commonly in a dried form. The fruit is dried then compressed into blocks (usually available in 1 lb (450 g) blocks wrapped in cellophane in the Indian delicatessen). It is quite sticky and contains husks and large pips. Tamarind is used in Indian cookery as a souring agent, especially in South India. The flavour is unique and very sour indeed. Lemon or vinegar, which can be used as substitutes, will give completely different flavours.

To prepare it, pour a small amount of boiling water over a piece of tamarind, broken off the main block. Wait for the water to cool, then rub and squash it, and work it around thoroughly until a purée is formed. Then the fibres, husks and seeds can be sieved away.

Oils

Edible oil and fat can be produced from many vegetables and from meat, fish, poultry etc. It can also be produced from milk in the form of butter. Many Indian dishes are cooked in oil, and the type traditionally used depends on the region the dish comes from.

In this country we can get many suitable oils, and only the better restaurants bother with anything other than cheap vegetable oil. I have tried many recipes using the prescribed oil and quite honestly I find it makes very little difference what you use. For deep-frying I use a good quality odourless corn oil. This will do for all your Indian cookery actually, but for added interest I also use mustard oil which gives a distinctive flavour to the more delicate Southern Indian dishes. It is made from mustard seeds and smells a bit strong until it is cooked, when it becomes quite sweet in flavour. A light oil – sunflower oil, for example – is superb for lightly stir-fried vegetable dishes. It is odourless and is ideal in that it does not affect delicate and subtle dishes.

Ghee (pronounced with a hard G as in geese) is clarified butter or margarine and is much used in the North. It has a wonderful flavour and really improves things like parathas or pullao rice and some curries. It is expensive to buy in tins but easy to make (see page 33).

Other more esoteric oils include palm oil, coconut oil, almond, peanut (and virtually all nuts), fish oil etc. I do not bother with any of these.

One oil you should *never* use in any Indian cooking is olive oil. It imparts a strong flavour which does not go at all well with Indian cuisine.

Special Fresh Ingredients

These are the ones which you may not normally keep in stock – garlic, ginger, onions, fresh coriander, mint and coconut.

GARLIC

It is best to buy one or more bulbs on which are clustered a number of individual cloves. The skin is discarded and you should be left with a creamy, plump firm clove.

To use, I prefer to chop the cloves finely (you can use a spring vegetable chopper), but you can use a garlic crusher (I think these are messy to clean and wasteful), or simply crush them under the flat side of a knife blade. To purée garlic, use an electric food processor or mortar and pestle.

Indian restaurants often use large quantities of garlic powder in place of real garlic which saves a lot of time. It also helps to capture that distinctive restaurant flavour, assisted no doubt by the sulphur dioxide and chemical stabilisers it contains. It also seems to cause dehydration. How often have you woken during the night with a raging thirst after eating an Indian restaurant curry? Real garlic does not seem to do that. If you do use garlic powder use 2 teaspoons for every clove specified in the recipe. Sometimes I like to use powder and sometimes fresh, and yet again a combination can be interesting.

If you and your friends like garlic add more (a lot more if you like) to the recipes. If you are worried about what it will do to your career, your social or love life, you can cut down on the quantities or omit it altogether.

GINGER

Ginger is a rhizome or root which grows underground, and is native to Asia and other suitable climates. It comes in three forms – fresh, whole dried, and as powder. Fresh is the best way, and it stays fresh for many months after being cropped. It is readily available at UK greengrocers. Size is not always a guide to quality. It should look plump, not withered, and have a pinky beige skin with a slight sheen. When cut the ginger should be a primrose-cream colour with no sign at all of blue or staleness. It is not possible to tell if it is stale until you cut it, so if you know your greengrocer well, ask him to cut it before you buy it. It should not be stringy or very dry and tough.

To use, you must peel off all the skin using a potato peeler. Then chop it, slice it or purée it as you choose, or as the recipe suggests, where in fact I have not specified that you peel the fresh ginger – I just assume that you will!

Some restaurants save a lot of work by using ginger powder. Some of the recipes in this book do use powder but there is really no substitute for fresh.

Ginger is quite hot and pungent so do not over-do the quantity unless you are a ginger freak.

It is worth mentioning that *turmeric* is another rhizome related to ginger. It is *always* used in powder form which saves us all a lot of hard work, but watch out for it in chunks in some Indian pickles.

ONION

Onions in India are relatively small, quite hot and with pink skins. They are not available in the UK but small English or, better, French, have a similar flavour. Of course the smaller they are the more work there is in peeling them, and the hotter they are the more you'll cry. The restaurants prefer to use the large mild Spanish ones and so do I. These give you a good consistency for puréeing, and heat can quickly be added with chilli powder. Some restaurants use dehydrated onion flakes which is the least labour intensive, though dearest, way of preparing onions. Keep fresh onions in the light or they will sprout green leaves and be useless. (Potatoes, on the other hand, must be kept in the dark to prevent sprouting.)

FRESH CORIANDER

Fresh green coriander is one of the great additives to curries, and gives a delicious taste when used as a garnish or added towards the end of cooking. It is increasingly available at good supermarkets and at Continental and Indian grocers' shops. The leaves only are used; the stalks are a little bitter and are discarded (although guinea pigs and rabbits adore them, so if you or your friends or their kids...).

Fresh parsley can be substituted if you can't get coriander, which does not taste the same, but *looks* nice. Gardeners will probably be able to grow coriander but things like that are above and beyond me. Fresh coriander will last about a week if kept in water (change it daily). You can also freeze it chopped, in ice cubes, for adding to curries prior to serving.

FRESH MINT

Fresh mint appears in some Indian recipes. This is readily available in season, and easy to grow in pots or in the garden. You can freeze it as with coriander, or bottle it in vinegar (no sugar) for use out of season.

COCONUT

Coconut can be obtained in a variety of forms in the UK. Best of all, but fairly hard work, is fresh coconut. Everyone knows those brown hairy objects from the fairground, and they are regularly available from many greengrocers or supermarkets. Using them presents a few problems, though.

Firstly, which do you buy? Simply shake them, when you should hear a good squishy sound of liquid. Dry ones are useless. Look at the whole nut. Be sure it looks fresh with no mould, especially around the two black 'eyes'.

Next one has to open them up. I usually rub them with a scrubbing brush to remove loose dust and hairs, then rinse them and clear away all dirt and hairs around the eyes. Then I remove the liquid. This is the coconut water (not coconut milk). I use a large 6 inch (15 cm) clean nail and a hammer and make one hole in each eye. Drain the liquid out into a glass or bowl and reserve for future use.

Next halve it (I use a hack-saw). A serrated bread knife can do it, but it is more difficult. Or simply use a hammer and break it into random pieces. Then cut away the coconut flesh from the dark outer skin. Grate, chop or grind down the flesh.

To make coconut milk, simmer the grated flesh with an equal quantity of water for 20 minutes, stirring frequently. Add water if necessary. Strain, reserve the liquid and repeat the process with new water. Strain the second batch combining it with the first and discard the flesh or use it in cooking. The coconut water can be used as a vegetable stock, and the milk to enhance the flavour of any curry using coconut.

Using fresh coconut calls for hard work but the flavour is better than the alternatives. You can use desiccated coconut instead of fresh, to make milk as above. Or you can use creamed coconut blocks which come in 4 oz (115 g) packets. Cut off a chunk and melt it down with the other ingredients. Tinned coconut milk is also available.

Equipment

Indian cuisine has been around for centuries and, traditionally, its preparation is a devoted and time-consuming job. Even today the old methods are the only methods in the villages and smaller towns in the curry lands, where electricity and running water are unknown, and time is unlimited. Fortunately the meal we get using modern appliances is indistinguishable from one prepared the old way and all Curry Club recipes use the simplest and most effective method to obtain the final result. Perhaps there is one area where traditional methods are best, and that is the tandoor or clay oven, usually dug several feet into the ground and fired by charcoal. Gas or electric ovens just do not match the flavour of tandoori-style cooking (but that's not to say the results we get are poor).

Most kitchens will already have the tools and pans we need. But these are items that are particularly important:

Frying pan
Deep-frier (a pan with a basket, or electric deep-friers are wonderful)
Large saucepan(s)
Two or three smaller non-stick pans
Large casserole(s)
Chinese-style wok (the Indian version, known as the karahi, is very useful for all types of Indian cooking)
Large sieve
Large slotted spoon for use in deep-frier
Cutting knives and board

Many of the recipes in this book can be prepared using a pressure cooker or a microwave. For those used to these tools it will be easy to modify the recipes to suit.

Further useful tools are either a coffee grinder to grind spices and/or a mortar and pestle. The newer electric food processors are also very handy labour savers. Electric blenders and attachments are useful although not essential. The sprung-type mechanical vegetable choppers save work and are very much cheaper than the electric equivalents.

A barbecue is a great asset in the summer.

Keeping Curry

Some people say that the historical origin of using spices in food was to mask the unpleasant taste of ingredients which were prone to 'going off' very quickly in hot countries. I don't know how true this is, but no amount of spicing will disguise bad ingredients. Equally, whilst currying may be one way to use up left-overs, you cannot expect your 'left-over' curry to be as good as one made with fresh ingredients. Only absolutely fresh and top quality ingredients, prepared and cooked as soon as possible, will produce top quality curries.

As a general rule, any meat, poultry, seafood or fish curry can be served immediately after cooking, or a few hours later, or even a day or two later. The taste and texture of the dish will change as marination takes place, and it's up to you which you prefer. Vegetables, in my opinion, taste better served straight after cooking, but they too will keep. Lentils improve with keeping after cooking, but rice does not, although you will get away with keeping rice for a day or maybe more. Chutneys should always be fresh.

Common sense must prevail when keeping any food. Keep it away from warmth, preferably in a fridge. Use a cover or cling-film, and do not use if you even suspect it may be going off. 48 hours is a long time for any dish to sit around and freezing is a much safer method of storing.

Freezing

Technically you can freeze any curry and rice, indeed many of the recipes in this book. Refer to a good freezing book for further details. Freezing will change the taste of a curry – it's like a long marination. It will soften meats and vegetables and tends to intensify whole aromatic spices like cloves, cardamoms and cassia bark. You may prefer to remove these items before freezing.

Do *not* freeze if the food has been kept warm for a long time or reheated, especially chicken. There is a risk of infection. And always use frozen curries within three months.

Disasters

Every chef or cook has a disaster at some time, and it always seems to come at the worst possible time – usually because one's attention has wandered – and suddenly one is gripped with panic and a ruined meal. I heard recently of a major restaurant kitchen which actually caught fire during the night's peak. The kitchen staff doused the fire and with the fire brigade in attendance calmly carried on re-cooking the meals with only a minimal hold-up and without any diners realising anything had happened. Most dramas at home are not so devastating and most mistakes can be corrected. Here are some methods for the most obvious.

TO MAKE A THICK SAUCE THINNER

In most cases simply add water – but just a little at a time. It may help to add oil as well, at a lower ratio – four times water to one of oil, for instance. This will retain the body of the dish. Cook for several minutes before serving to ensure blending.

TO MAKE A THIN SAUCE THICKER

Either ladle off the excess liquid into a reserve pan, or if there really is a lot of liquid, strain the entire dish. Continue to cook the drier dish until it blends and add back some of the reserved liquid if needed.

If in a hurry you can quickly thicken a runny sauce by using rice flour. It does not have the wheaty taste of ordinary flour but too much will alter the taste of your curry. Use in emergency only.

TOO OILY

Remove the dish from the heat. Let it stand until the oil floats to the top. Ladle the oil off (keep it for subsequent cooking), stir well and reheat.

UNDER-COOKED MEAT

Nothing for it but to cook it some more. Avoid this, if the occasion is important, by cooking the main meat dish(es) either earlier on in the day or the day before, and letting it/them stand while everything else is prepared.

Always have appetisers on hand for your guests to allow yourself breathing space. As long as people are picking at something, they are happy – and they are less likely to notice you panicking in the kitchen!

COLOUR

There is nothing less appetising than grey-looking curries and dhals. Your principal ingredients will define the colour you *should* get but you may want to enhance it. The simple trick is food colouring. Red, orange, yellow and green powders are immensely effective, and the merest pinch will do the trick. Try for example, ⅛ teaspoon of yellow in your next dhal (see page 120). For those few people who dislike these additives or are allergic to them, you can use turmeric (yellow), paprika (red), ground spinach (green), or alkenet root (deep crimson). Although natural, these are less effective than powders and they do change the flavour of your dish. To go darker (browner) use soy sauce or gravy browning (meat extract).

TOO SOUR

Add white or brown sugar, or a sweetish sauce (tomato sauce for example) or puréed mango chutney. Just a spoonful or two should pull back the over-sour taste. Try it bit by bit, stirring and tasting as you go.

TOO SWEET

This is a trifle harder to rectify. You can add a souring agent such as lemon juice, vinegar or tamarind, but this will probably change the flavour of the dish. If you have time try adding something which will 'spread' the taste, such as frozen peas. You can then quickly fry up a second spicing with onions to add to the mix. If you have plenty of time, make a new batch omitting all things sweet which caused the initial problem. Combine the two when cooked and freeze the surplus.

TOO SALTY

It is infinitely better to under-salt – even to omit it altogether. Diners can easily sprinkle their own at the table and it never affects the quality of the dish to do so. However, most of us like to add at least a little salt while cooking and it is then that mistakes can happen. If it is gross – the salt pot burst and flooded into the dish! – do not stir, quickly ladle out the salt from the area where it sits or gently spoon it off the top. If it is stirred in and is just a case of slight over-salting, simply omit salt from everything else. If it is too late for that and the principal dish is the only problem you can add quick items – frozen peas or other vegetables, tinned items like tomatoes etc – anything to bulk out the taste. If there is a bit more time fry yourself some onions and spices to make a thick gravy and add it to your dish. If it is the day before make a second batch and combine it with the first, freezing the surplus.

CURDLING

All milk-based products – milk, cream, yoghurt etc – are prone to curdling when heated and added to acidic ingredients. Lightly beating the cream or yoghurt, or shaking the milk in its bottle or carton, ensures adequate mixing. When adding to ingredients already cooking, reducing the heat to cool also reduces the risk of curdling. If the worst does occur, though, strain the contents of your pan, cool then add some more of the same ingredient (cream, yoghurt or milk) and reheat, then add back the strained liquid as required. Stir continuously until you reach cooking heat.

BURNING

The worst disaster and all too easy to happen, and if it is very bad you have no alternative but to dispose of the offending item. But *prevention* is the answer. If your dish is very dry keep stirring. If you are grilling watch it all the time. If the contents of a pan stick, *do not stir*: remove the pan from the heat, let it cool down, then stir, when the sticking will release if it is minor. If it has actually burned, very gently turn out the contents when cool and carefully separate all burned food. If the whole dish tastes lightly of carbon (burnt taste), you may be able to rectify by adding sweetness (see *Too sour*).

Serving and Dining

Part of the fun of Indian food is the serving. This is best done by placing the curries, rice and dhals into metal or porcelain serving bowls and placing them in the centre of the table so that diners help themselves. Chutneys and pickles are attractive in little side bowls with teaspoons. Eat on dinner plates with dessertspoon and fork. Knives are only useful to cut bread. Provide a side plate for bread when you serve it. Don't be afraid to use your fingers – especially for Tandoori Chicken etc. After all, using fingers (of the right hand) is the polite and traditional way. In India even the most exclusive society is happy using fingers, and it was a recent Persian Royal Shah who said 'eating with a knife and fork is like making love through an interpreter'.

Normally with the main course one would expect to serve a side dish and/or a bread, a main dish and maybe one or two secondary dishes plus a number of chutneys and pickles. For a big party, you can increase the number of dishes. In the days of the Moghul emperors, the number of dishes you served indicated your wealth and prestige, so it was quite common for a banquet to contain hundreds of dishes and last for days. I doubt that you'll want to emulate that, but I'm sure you'll want to try a big feast at least once – it's ideal for parties because so much can be prepared in advance.

A SIMPLE MENU

Here is a suggestion for a very simple menu for 4 people:

Aperitif	8 Papadams (page 16)
Starter	10 Onion Bhajias (page 43)

Main Course	Medium Chicken Curry (page 84)
	Dhal (page 120)
Accompaniments	Plain Basmati Rice (page 122)
	Fresh Onion Chutney (page 145)
	Fresh Cucumber Raita (page 140)
	Mango Chutney (page 152)
	Lime Pickle (bottled)
Dessert	Fresh fruit, ice cream or Kulfi (page 162)
Coffee	Chocolate mints

If you invite guests for this meal it would be a good idea to practise it on the family beforehand. As you get more confident you'll probably become more adventurous.

One word of warning which may sound obvious here, but could be embarrassing 'on the night'. If you are inviting new guests and you do not know whether they eat spicy foods, the best advice I can give is 'don't'. Nothing is worse for hosts and guests than having a guest struggling with a disliked food. So don't serve curry at all. Play safe and invite only those whom you know will enjoy it. Then you'll all have a ball.

DRINKS WITH THE MEAL

Quite often you hear one or another expert declaring that it is quite wrong to drink alcoholic beverages with Indian-style food. It is rubbish, of course. Drink whatever takes your fancy – drink is for pleasure, not the rule book. True, some Indian religions, particularly Moslem and some Hindu, preclude the drinking of alcohol, and in many Indian states there is prohibition. But there is a thriving Indian beer and wine industry and spirits are distilled there too. Local concoctions such as feni from Goa and toddy are fierce and knock you out.

Light drinks such as lager, cider, white wine or rosé go very well with curries. Red wine and spirits are possibly too strong for subtle spicing – and heavy spicing is too strong for subtle wines. It's horses for courses.

The traditional Indian beverages with the meal are fresh lime or yoghurt (lhassi), and I include recipes for these in Chapter 10.

It is always a good idea to have a jug of iced water on the table. It's not that the food is so hot that you need to gulp it down – in fact dieticians say it is wrong to drink too much during a meal – but it is very refreshing, and clears the palate from time to time.

My extravagant favourite beverage with curry is champagne if the occasion warrants it (and any excuse will do). Blow the expense … pink or white, not too dry. It just goes brilliantly with curry. Cheers!

AFTER THE MEAL

Wherever you go in India you will find people eating paan. In some of the Asian communities in Britain you can now obtain paan and the raw ingredients to make it – supari. Some restaurants over here offer it, but beware, it is a highly acquired taste.

So what is paan? Basically it is a combination of sweet, sour and bitter tastes wrapped in a small dark green heart-shaped leaf (paan leaf) folded to a triangular shape and pinned with a clove. It looks delightful. The mixture of 'tastes' is the paan masala or supari. It includes any combination of lime paste, date paste, tobacco, shredded betel nut, aniseeds, cardamoms, sugar balls, coconut, pistachio nuts and melon and cucumber seeds. The whole paan is popped into the mouth after the meal and munched until it has gone. It aids the digestion and sweetens the breath.

Some restaurants offer just the supari mix, which to those not accustomed to whole paans is easier to eat.

2
BASIC COOKING TECHNIQUES

No-one is quite certain when Indian-style cooking began. It is lost in the realms of pre-recorded history. There is certainly evidence that it pre-dates the Pharaohs and that takes it back some 7,000 years. For most of those years it has developed and been handed from mother to daughter, cook to cook, father to son and chef to chef by word of mouth and by example. In the Indian sub-continent today it is still the way most information is handed on, and it is only very recently that anyone has thought to write down the thousands of recipes – and the many cooking techniques – which are so well known to Asians.

Curry Techniques

It's a funny thing about curry – it doesn't exist! The word simply does not appear in any of the fifteen or so languages on the Indian sub-continent. There is no translation for the word either and many an Indian has no idea what you mean when you talk about curry. Yet say the word to your average Brit and it conjures up a dish, a meal, a feast – indeed, the whole continent of India. There are various theories as to how the word derived (see Glossary).

The main thing we cooks have to worry about is to achieve the correct mixture and preparation of spices for a particular dish, and the correct texture. The actual selection of spices is less important than what you do with them. This section tells you the very important initial stages of making a curry. Whatever else you do, master these techniques and you will be assured of good curries for ever after. These are the stages:

The Masala (the spice mixture)
The Paste (of the spice mixture)
The Bhoona (the frying of the spice mixture)
The Bargar (frying whole spices)
The Purée (of onion and/or garlic and/or ginger)
Marinating

THE MASALA

The Spice Mixture

It is the combination of spices which makes Indian-style cooking so distinctive. This combination is known in Hindi as the masala or spice mixture, a word you will come across often in the Indian restaurant or cookbook. In this book we refer to the masala as spices, except garam masala (hot mixture) which has a very specific meaning (see page 31). In many recipes it is vital in curry cooking to pre-cook the masala spices by frying before combining with the main ingredients. This operation is easy to do and is fully explained in each relevant recipe throughout the book. The Indian term for this is 'bhoona' (or the spice fry).

THE PASTE

Of the Spice Mixture

To ensure a cohesive mixture of ground spices a paste is usually made using water (sometimes vinegar, as with Vindaloo). The water prevents the spices from burning up when they are introduced to the oil in the bhoona process.

1 Select a mixing bowl large enough to enable you to stir the masala.
2 Stir the masala until it is fully mixed.
3 Add enough water *and no more* to form a stiff paste.
4 Leave it to stand for a minimum of 10 minutes. It does not matter how *long* it stands. This ensures the ground spices absorb all the water.
5 Add a little water if it is too dry prior to using in the bhoona process.

THE BHOONA

The bhoona is the Hindi term for the process of cooking the spice paste in hot oil. This is an important part of the curry cooking process which removes the raw taste of the spices and influences the final taste of the dish. Use the bhoona method whenever the recipes in this book state that you should 'fry the spices'. In fact, traditionally you should fry the spice paste first then add the puréed or chopped onion second. This method can easily cause burned spices so I reverse this process and I have found that it works very satisfactorily.

1 Take a round-sided pan such as a karahi or wok. If you don't have one, use an ordinary frying pan (a non-stick one is best).
2 Heat the oil to quite a high heat (but not smoking).
3 Remove the pan from the heat and at once gently add the onion purée. Return to the heat and commence stirring.
4 *From this point do not let your attention wander.* Keep stirring the purée until the oil is hot again then gently add the masala paste. Beware of splattering.
5 Keep stirring. The water in the paste lowers the temperature. Do not let the mixture stick at all. Do not stop stirring, not even for a few seconds.
6 After a few minutes the water will have evaporated out and the oil will float above the mixture. The spices will be cooked. Remove the pan from the heat. Proceed with the remainder of the recipe.

THE BARGAR

Some of the recipes in this book require you to fry whole spices. The process is for the same reason as the bhoona – to cook out the raw taste from the spices. Again the oil should be hot, and the spices are put into the oil with no water or purée. You must use your judgement as to when they are cooked. Do not let them blacken. As soon as they begin to change colour or to float they are ready. It will not take more than a couple of minutes.

If you do burn the bhoona or bargar process you must throw the result away and start again. Better to waste a small amount of spices than a whole meal.

THE PURÉE

An onion purée is the basis for nearly all curries. One way of cutting down on time and energy is to make a large batch at one time. This recipe will make enough purée for ten curries to feed four people each time. You can decide for yourself whether to make more or less. You can also leave out the garlic and/or ginger, or do them separately, and freeze.

10 large onions   **4 oz (115 g) fresh ginger, peeled**
20 large cloves of garlic   **1 pint (600 ml) vegetable oil**

1 Coarsely chop all the vegetables, and heat half the oil in a saucepan.
2 Add the onion, garlic and ginger and fry for 15 minutes or so (until very soft and translucent, but not browning). Leave to cool.
3 Purée in a food processor when cool, and heat the remaining oil.
4 Fry the purée for at least 15 minutes, ensuring it does not stick.
5 Cool, then pour into ten yoghurt pots. Freeze.

Makes: enough for 10 curries

MARINATING

Even today in India and the sub-continent meat and poultry is not only expensive but it is often tough and stringy. To overcome this, marinade techniques have been developed, using yoghurt, lemon juice, vinegar, even wine, and the meat can be left in these for anything from 1 to 3 days. Where a marinade is necessary, it is explained in the recipe.

Curry Spice Mixture

By now, I'm sure that you will have gathered that as far as I'm concerned, commercial curry powder is **out** for cooking a respectable Indian-style meal. However, there are one or two preparations which are useful to make up in bulk (any combination of ground spices listed in these recipes can in fact be made up in bulk if you like a dish – it saves time – then you have your own individual curry powder! Do not make up any more than you are likely to use in 3 months or so, as after that they start to go stale.

GARAM MASALA

Garam means hot and masala means mixture of spices and there are as many combinations and recipes of garam masala as there are cooks who make it. Some use only five or six spices and I have one recipe which lists as many as fifteen spices! This one has only nine and has been my favourite for years. Try it. For the next batch, you might like to vary the mixture to your own preference. That's the fun of Indian cookery. (I list in metric only, as that's the only way I weigh out the spices for this, and it doesn't transfer easily into Imperial.)

110 g coriander seeds	**30 g cardamoms, brown**
110 g cummin seeds	**15 g nutmeg**
50 g black peppercorns	**10 g bay leaves**
30 g cassia bark	**15 g ground ginger**
30 g cloves	

1 Lightly roast everything except the ground ginger under a low to medium heat grill, or in an oven at about 325°F (160°C) Gas 3. Do not let the spices burn. They should give off a light steam.

2 When they give off an aroma – in the oven, 10 minutes is enough – remove from the heat, cool and grind. A coffee grinder will do if you use small quantities, and break up large items first.

3 After grinding add the ground ginger, mix thoroughly and store in an airtight jar. Garam masala will last almost indefinitely, but it is always better to make small fresh batches every few months to get the best flavours.

This particular garam masala is available from The Curry Club.

TANDOORI MIX POWDER

If you are a tandoori fan, it is a good idea to make up a batch of tandoori mix powder for use as and when you need it (see Chapter 4). This makes about 8 oz (225 g) which is enough for eight to ten tandoori dishes for four, or thirty-two to forty individual portions!

3½ tablespoons paprika

3½ tablespoons coriander, ground

3½ tablespoons cummin, ground

2½ tablespoons ground ginger

2 teaspoons orange food colouring powder (optional)

Mix the spices thoroughly in a bowl then keep in a screw-top jar, or a plastic container, out of sunlight.

PANCH PHORAN

This is a Bengali mixture of five (panch) spices. There are several possible combinations. This is my favourite. Use it in vegetable cooking – for example, the Carrot, Peas and Nut Curry in Chapter 7.
Mix together equal parts – a teaspoon of each is plenty – of:

white cummin seeds

fennel seeds

fenugreek seeds

mustard seeds

wild onion seeds

Ghee, Stock and Curry Gravies

Ghee is expensive to buy, but it's simplicity itself to make at home, and it keeps for almost ever. Its flavour contributes enormously to any recipe that uses it. As does stock, which is always better than water in a sauce or soup, and can be kept in the freezer. The gravy recipes can also be kept in the freezer for almost 'instant' use. They are useful as accompaniments, or you can serve pre-cooked meat, fish or vegetables in them.

GHEE

I have already mentioned ghee in the Oils section of the last chapter. It is a clarified butter, which is very easy to make and gives a distinctive and delicious taste. When cooled and set, it will keep for several months without refrigeration.

**2 lb (900 g) slightly salted
   butter**

I Place the butter blocks whole into a medium non-stick pan. Melt at a very low heat.

2 When completely melted, raise heat very slightly. Ensure it does not smoke or burn, but don't stir. Leave to cook for about 1 hour. The impurities will sink to the bottom and float on the top. Carefully skim off the floating sediment with a slotted spoon, but don't touch the bottom.

3 Turn off the heat and allow ghee to cool a little. Then sieve it through kitchen paper or muslin into an airtight storage jar. When it cools it solidifies, although it is quite soft. It should be a bright pale lemon colour and it smells like toffee. If it has burned it will be darker and smell different. Providing it is not too burned it can still be used.

STOCK

If you have a stock to hand it will always give your dish a nicer taste than simply using water. I always keep stocks in the fridge or freezer.

To make a vegetable stock, retain any water in which you have boiled vegetables (full of goodness like minerals and trace elements). Each time you boil fresh vegetables you can use your existing stock. It will both enhance the flavour of the vegetables being boiled and the stock. You can keep it in the fridge for a couple of days – but it is essential to re-boil it after 2 days. It will be safe for several re-boils, but use it finally in a soup or other cooking. Add the brine or water from tinned vegetables to your stock.

To make a meat stock, simmer bones, fresh left-overs, scraps of meat etc, in boiling water for an hour or so. Strain and discard the solids. Keep the stock in the fridge for not more than 24 hours. Re-boil before using in soup or other cooking.

Don't be frightened of adding to any stock. The normal flavouring agents are onions, bay leaves, carrots, peppercorns, a herb or parsley, and anything (if not too spicy) will make its contribution to the richness and ultimate flavour of the stock.

PAKISTANI CURRY GRAVY

This is a remarkable recipe supplied by Ivan Watson. Its 'cunning' lies in the fact that the milk is coagulated by the tomatoes and provides smooth homogenous 'solids', floating in the oil.

1 cup milk
6 tablespoons vegetable oil
14 oz (400 g) tin tomatoes, strained
1 teaspoon sugar
salt

Spices 1
1 teaspoon chilli powder
4 teaspoons coriander, ground
3 teaspoons turmeric
4 teaspoons garlic powder

Spices 2
4 teaspoons paprika
1 teaspoon garam masala
1 teaspoon dry fenugreek leaves

SP *Spice pack available*

1 Mix *spices 1* with a little of the milk into a paste, and heat oil on a low heat. Put the paste into the oil and fry gently for a few minutes, stirring once or twice. Remove from heat and cool a bit.

2 Liquidise the tomatoes in a blender, and stir into the fried paste. Return to heat. Add sugar, salt and remaining milk. Stir continuously.

3 When solids start to separate from the oil, add *spices 2*. If the sauce is a little too thick, add a little more milk.

4 Add pre-cooked meats, chicken, vegetables or frozen seafood, and simmer until ready.

Serves: 4 or more

SAVOURY CURRY GRAVY ✓ pc

12 tablespoons corn oil
2 large onions, very finely
  chopped
4-6 cloves garlic, very finely
  chopped
water
1 tablespoon tomato purée
1 tablespoon tomato ketchup
salt

Spices

2 teaspoons turmeric
2 teaspoons cummin, ground
1 teaspoon chilli powder
1 teaspoon coriander, ground
1 teaspoon garam masala
4 teaspoons paprika
2 teaspoons dry fenugreek
  leaves

SP **Spice pack available**

1 Heat oil and fry onion and garlic until they are golden.

2 Mix *spices* into ¼ pint (150 ml) water, and add to onion. Cook for a further 5–10 minutes.

3 Reduce heat to simmer. Add tomato purée and ketchup and more water, then simmer for half an hour or so. Keep adding water to stop it getting too dry.

4 Add pre-cooked meat or chicken, or frozen seafood and salt, and further chilli powder if you want it very hot. Add water as necessary, and keep simmering until you want to serve it.

Serves: *4 or more*

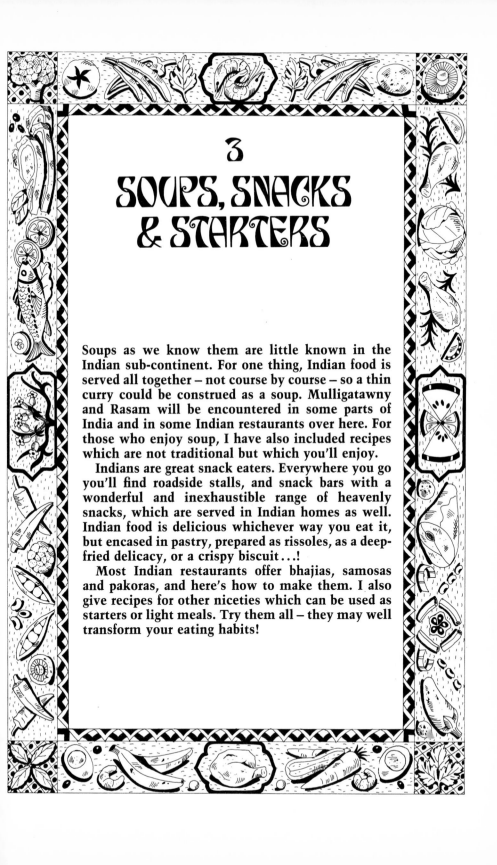

3
SOUPS, SNACKS & STARTERS

Soups as we know them are little known in the Indian sub-continent. For one thing, Indian food is served all together – not course by course – so a thin curry could be construed as a soup. Mulligatawny and Rasam will be encountered in some parts of India and in some Indian restaurants over here. For those who enjoy soup, I have also included recipes which are not traditional but which you'll enjoy.

Indians are great snack eaters. Everywhere you go you'll find roadside stalls, and snack bars with a wonderful and inexhaustible range of heavenly snacks, which are served in Indian homes as well. Indian food is delicious whichever way you eat it, but encased in pastry, prepared as rissoles, as a deep-fried delicacy, or a crispy biscuit...!

Most Indian restaurants offer bhajias, samosas and pakoras, and here's how to make them. I also give recipes for other niceties which can be used as starters or light meals. Try them all – they may well transform your eating habits!

MULLIGATAWNY SOUP

*Mulligatawny is a Sri-Lankan dish, from the Tamil words molegoo
(pepper) and tunee (water). It accompanies rice and dry curries, but it
also makes an excellent soup. The original version was vegetarian, as
is this recipe. Meat eaters can use meat stock and small pieces of
chicken or meat in addition to the ingredients listed.*

1½ pints (900 ml) meat or
vegetable stock or
2 × 14 fl oz (400 ml) tins
clear consommé + water

1 medium onion, very finely
chopped

1 clove garlic, very finely
chopped

1 tablespoon ghee

2 green chillies, very finely
chopped (optional)

1 tablespoon rice, cooked

2 tablespoons tamarind juice
(see page 16)

salt

Spices

½ teaspoon mustard seeds

½ teaspoon fenugreek seeds

½ teaspoon turmeric

½ teaspoon cummin, ground

½ teaspoon coriander, ground

1 teaspoon black pepper,
ground

1 Heat the stock or consommé (or combination), gently.

2 Meanwhile, fry the onion and garlic in the ghee until golden, then
add the *spices* and cook for a further 3–5 minutes.

3 Combine all the ingredients and simmer for 10–15 minutes. Salt to
taste, then serve very hot.

Serves: 4

SPICY TOMATO SOUP

Simple to make, and delicious to taste, this is a spicy adaptation of a favourite British soup.

2 pints (generous litre) water or vegetable stock, or tinned tomato juice, or combination

10 fresh tomatoes (can be quite over-ripe) or 14 oz (397 g) tin

1 onion, chopped

4 cloves garlic, chopped

1 tablespoon Worcestershire sauce

1 tablespoon tomato ketchup

1 tablespoon tomato purée

salt

Spices

1 teaspoon cummin, ground

½ teaspoon wild onion seeds

1 teaspoon sesame seeds

1 teaspoon chilli powder (optional)

1 Boil the water or stock, then add the tomatoes, onion and garlic.

2 Make a paste of the spices with water, and add to the pot. Simmer for about 30 minutes.

3 *If you want a thin soup,* add the Worcestershire sauce, tomato ketchup and purée, and salt to taste. Serve when ready, with the vegetable pieces floating in the soup.

4 *If you want a thick soup,* after adding the spices to the stock and vegetables, put the mixture through a blender, processor or sieve. Simmer for 10–15 more minutes. Add the Worcestershire sauce, tomato ketchup and purée. Serve, garnished with cream and parsley.

Serves: *6*

Moong dhal consommé

Dhal (or lentils) is so nutritious and filling. Try this soup for a tasty supper dish.

2 oz (50 g) moong dhal
½ cup tomato juice or
    vegetable stock

½ clove garlic, finely chopped
6 black peppercorns, crushed
salt

1 Boil dhal in 1 pint (600 ml) water until well cooked, then mash to a fine purée (electrically, or by hand).

2 Add 2 pints (generous litre) water, along with the tomato juice or stock, garlic and pepper. Simmer for at least 10 minutes.

3 Strain off the solids and discard, then reheat the soup. Salt to taste, and serve garnished with coriander leaves or parsley.

Serves: *4–6*

Chilli soup

This concoction is not authentic. It is pure invention, and for hot heads like myself! Do not offer it to anyone unused to chilli heat!

1 cup fresh green chillies, de-
    stalked and chopped, or red
    dry chillies (keep seeds)
1 lb (450 g) tinned or fresh
    tomatoes
1 large onion, chopped
4 cloves garlic, chopped
1 inch (2.5 cm) fresh ginger,
    chopped
1 green pepper, chopped and
    de-seeded (optional)
salt

Spices
1 teaspoon mustard seeds
1 tablespoon dry fenugreek
    leaves
1 teaspoon mustard powder

1 Boil 2½ pints (1.5 litres) water, and add all the ingredients. Simmer for a minimum of 30 minutes, maximum 1 hour.

2 Strain, if you want to serve as a consommé, or you can serve it as it is, with the vegetables.

3 Or you can purée the soup after cooking. Simmer for a further 20 minutes minimum.

4 Salt both soups to taste, and a final touch can be achieved by adding any bottled chilli sauce (Tabasco, for instance) to taste.

Serves: 4–6

RASAM

A traditional pepper soup from South India, which should be served piping hot.

1 tablespoon split moong dhal

2 tablespoons tamarind pulp (see page 16)

1 tablespoon mustard oil

1 small onion, finely chopped

2 cloves garlic, chopped

1 tomato, roughly chopped

1 tablespoon fresh grated or desiccated coconut

4 fresh red chillies, finely chopped

salt

1 tablespoon finely chopped fresh coriander

Spices

1 teaspoon mustard seeds

1 teaspoon cummin seeds

1 teaspoon black peppercorns

1 dessertspoon curry leaves

1 Boil the dhal in 2 cups water until tender, about 30 minutes. Boil the tamarind at the same time in 1 cup water for 10 minutes, then sieve and discard husks.

2 Heat the oil and fry the *spice* seeds until they pop, then add the onion, garlic, peppercorns and curry leaves. Fry for 10 minutes, then add the tomato and fry for a further 5 minutes.

3 Add the coconut, chillies, dhal and tamarind with 2 pints (generous litre) water, and boil for 10 minutes. Salt to taste.

4 Serve hot either sieved for clear soup, or as it comes, or puréed, and garnish with the fresh coriander.

Serves: 4–6

LEMON RASAM

A variation on the rasam theme, for there are many in South India. This one has a much sharper taste than the previous recipe.

½ cup toor or tovar dhal

1 inch (2.5 cm) fresh ginger, finely chopped

3 green chillies, finely chopped

½ cup lemon juice or PLJ

4 tablespoons tamarind juice (see page 16)

salt

1 tablespoon chopped fresh coriander

Spices

1 teaspoon cummin, ground

½ teaspoon black peppercorns

1 dessertspoon curry leaves

1 Boil the dhal until soft (35–40 minutes) in 1 pint (600 ml) water.

2 About half-way through, add the remaining ingredients and *spices*. Add water to keep it thin as necessary. Salt to taste.

3 Serve hot, either sieved as a clear soup, puréed, or as it comes. Garnish with the coriander.

Serves: 4–6

KADHI

This cold yoghurt soup is astonishingly simple to make, and very refreshing on hot summer days.

8 fl oz (225 ml) plain yoghurt

½ pint (300 ml) single cream

½ pint (300 ml) water

1 tablespoon chopped fresh mint

1 tablespoon chopped fresh coriander

3–4 inch (7.5–10 cm) piece cucumber

6 ice cubes

½ teaspoon ground black pepper

salt

paprika

Put everything in a blender and blend, or very finely chop and mix. Serve chilled, with some paprika sprinkled on top.

Serves: 4

ONION BHAJIAS

These are probably the most common starter to be found in Indian restaurants. You'll find them really quick and easy to make. It's just a matter of getting the batter consistency right. You must use gram flour (besan) which is made from channa dhal.

The two-stage cooking method in the recipe makes life easier if you want to serve bhajias at a dinner party.

2 large tablespoons gram flour
1 large onion, chopped into
    thin strips about 1 inch
    (2.5 cm) long
salt
corn oil for deep-frying

Spices
½ teaspoon turmeric
½ teaspoon cummin, ground
½ teaspoon garam masala
SP *Spice pack available*

1 Mix the *spices* thoroughly with the flour in a large bowl, then add a *little* water until the mixture is gluey. Mix the onion into the paste. Add a little salt.

2 Heat deep-frying oil to medium heat and gently drop a ping-pong-ball sized blob of mixture off a tablespoon into the hot fat. When it firms up (about half a minute), put in the next blob. Continue until the fryer is full. Cook about 10–15 minutes until golden brown. Drain on kitchen paper. You could serve them at this stage.

3 Or they can be allowed to cool. Reheat them in hot deep fat for about 2 minutes, but don't let them go too brown. Serve hot.

Makes: about 10

PAKORAS

To all intents and purposes, pakoras are the same thing as bhajias. They are also gram flour fritters, and are made in the same way. The main ingredient can be virtually anything. Try cauliflower florets, green pepper, chilli, potato cubes, aubergine, mushrooms, chicken or meat pieces or seafood. In each case cut to suitable sizes or strips. Do not pre-cook the main ingredient – even meat – as the deep-frying will cook it sufficiently. Try a mixture of ingredients for your next party.

SAMOSAS

The celebrated triangular mince or vegetable-filled patties. The instructions look complicated but it is well worth having a go. It takes a little practice to get a good shape which does not burst when deep-fried, but once you've got the hang of it, you'll be able to prepare them fairly easily. Reduce the ingredient quantities in proportion if you want to make fewer, or freeze those you don't want to eat straight away.

VEGETABLE SAMOSAS

corn oil
1 lb (450 g) strong white plain
  flour
2 lb (900 g) potatoes
4 teaspoons salt
1 lb (450 g) frozen peas

Spices
1 teaspoon black pepper,
  ground
2 teaspoons chilli powder
2 teaspoons coriander, ground
1 teaspoon cummin, ground
3 dessertspoons dry fenugreek
  leaves

SP *Spice pack available*

1 Add approximately 4 dessertspoons corn oil to the flour, and enough water to make a dough to leave the sides of the bowl clean. Leave to stand for at least 1 hour.

2 Boil potatoes, then mash and add *spices*, salt and the peas.

3 Make a flour and water paste (to glue samosas together) and put a little corn oil in a bowl (for easy access, when brushing discs at next stage).

4 Roll the rested dough into balls no smaller than 1½ inches (4 cm) in diameter, and roll out into discs of 4 inches (10 cm) in diameter (about 8 in all). Brush each disc with corn oil on one side. Sprinkle with flour and join two together, then roll *these* twin discs out to circles 8 inches (20 cm) in diameter.

5 While still hot cut the discs in half, then separate the two half pieces. Place each on working surface (a), and fold over one-third (b). Paste the top third with flour and water paste, then fold over the next third on top (c). You now have a cone shape.

6 Put filling mixture into cone (not too much), then fold over the top and seal with flour and water paste (d). Ensure whole samosa is very well sealed or it will burst while cooking. Use the paste liberally.

7 Deep-fry the samosas at medium heat for about 10–15 minutes, or until pale gold in colour. Don't over-cook or go too fast. Then let them rest for at least 10 minutes, or let them get cold. (You can freeze them at this stage.)

8 To finish off, grill slowly or deep-fry for a second time until golden brown.

Makes: 30

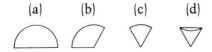

(a)   (b)   (c)   (d)

MEAT SAMOSAS

corn oil
1 lb (450 g) strong white plain
   flour
1 large onion, finely chopped
1 lb (450 g) lean minced meat
salt
1 lb (450 g) frozen peas

Spices
2 teaspoons coriander, ground
1 teaspoon cummin, ground
2 teaspoons turmeric
2 teaspoons chilli powder
1 teaspoon garam masala
1 dessertspoon dry fenugreek
   leaves

SP *Spice pack available*

1 Make dough as specified in Vegetable Samosa recipe, and leave to rest.

2 Heat a little corn oil in a pan and fry the chopped onion until golden. Fry the mince separately until brown, then drain off any juices.

3 Combine the onion, mince, a little salt and the *spices*, and cook gently for about 30 minutes. It should be fairly dry, and any liquid should be strained off. Leave to cool, then add peas.

4 Make dough discs and cones as in previous recipe (from No. 3), and stuff with cooled meat filling. Cook similarly, following Nos. 7 and 8.

Makes: 30

PRAWN BUTTERFLY

This dish has recently made its appearance on the Indian restaurant menu. It makes an ideal starter or snack and it is, in fact, a variation on the Pakora theme (page 43). Serve piping hot with a dip such as Tandoori Chutney (see page 143).

4 large king prawns or langoustines, fresh or frozen
2 tablespoons gram flour
2 tablespoons plain flour
1 teaspoon salt
water

Spices
1 teaspoon garam masala
1 teaspoon paprika

1 Mix the flour, salt and *spices* with enough water to form creamy dropping consistency.
2 Remove the shells and clean the prawns.
3 Heat a deep-frier to medium/hot.
4 Immerse the prawns in the batter.
5 Fry for about 10 minutes until the batter is a golden orange colour.

Serves: 4

PRAWN PURI

This is another new entrant to the restaurant starter menu. It is a combination of the Puri bread (see page 136) with small shrimps or prawn in the bread mix as well as in a garnish sauce.

one portion puri dough (see page 136)
4 oz (115 g) fresh shrimps or prawns
1 clove garlic, finely chopped
ghee or light vegetable oil
1 tablespoon tomato purée
salt
2 tablespoons chopped fresh coriander

Spices 1
1 teaspoon mustard seeds
1 teaspoon turmeric
1 teaspoon cummin, ground
½ teaspoon garam masala

1 Make the puri dough, mixing about 1 oz (25 g) of the de-shelled prawns into the dough. Allow it to stand for half an hour or more, then shape as in the puri recipe.

2 Meanwhile, fry the garlic and mustard seeds for 5 minutes in ghee or oil. Add the remaining prawns, tomato purée and ground spices, and fry for a further 5 minutes.

3 Deep-fry the puris. Serve very hot with the sauce on top. Garnish with fresh coriander and salt.

Makes: 8–10

PRAWN AND MUSHROOM CURRY VOL-AU-VENTS

A pure invention, I must confess. But why not? They taste delicious, and of course you can invent all manner of spicy fillings of your own.

ghee or melted butter

3–4 oz (75–115 g) button
  mushrooms

8 oz (225 g) peeled prawns

salt to taste

squeeze of lemon juice

14 oz (400 g) ready-made puff
  pastry, or packet vol-au-
  vent cases

Spices

1 generous teaspoon cummin
  seeds

½ teaspoon wild onion seeds
  (optional)

½ teaspoon chilli powder

1½ teaspoons turmeric

1 In a medium sized saucepan, fry the cummin and wild onion seeds very gently in the ghee.

2 Chop the mushrooms very finely and add them to the pan.

3 Add the chilli powder and turmeric, then the prawns. Mix well and cook gently for 2–3 minutes, stirring all the time.

4 Add salt to taste and a squeeze of lemon. Remove from the heat and allow to cool.

5 Cut the pastry into 2 inch (5 cm) vol-au-vent cases and bake as directed on the packet – usually at a temperature of about 425°F (200°C) Gas 7 – until golden. When cool, fill, and serve hot or cold.

Makes: about 25

CURRY PUFFS

I have never come across these in any Indian restaurant but I would be derelict in my duty if I did not bring them to your attention! The British community in India developed the recipe as a kind of variant on Cornish pasties or sausage rolls. You can make them to either shape – the recipe here is for the roll format – but both are stupendous!

14 oz (400 g) packet frozen puff pastry (or home-made)   **½ lb (225 g) meat or vegetable samosa filling (see pages 44 and 45)**

I Thaw pastry then cut into four equal pieces (a). Roll out each piece to ⅛ inch (3 mm) thickness, and cut into three 3 inch (7.5 cm) strips (b).

2 Taking one strip at a time, place a line of curry filling along the middle of the length of the strip (c).

3 Wet one long side of the strip with water and fold over the filling, sealing the edges, and cut each long roll into three 3 inch (7.5 cm) pieces (d). Brush with water, and spike each puff with knife to let out air. (Freeze now, if you like.)

4 Bake in fairly hot oven, at 425°F (220°C) Gas 7, for about 20 minutes, or until well browned. Serve hot or cold with chutneys.

Makes: 36

(a)   (b)

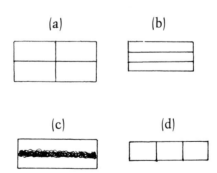

(c)   (d)

ALOO TIKI
Potato Chaps (Rissoles)

It's worth the effort to make this delicious recipe. Aloo tiki are vegetable rissoles, and are served traditionally with fresh mint and tamarind chutneys (see pages 143 and 146). Serve as a snack or a main course.

4 oz (115 g) channa dhal
salt
1 lb (450 g) potatoes, peeled
breadcrumbs
oil for frying

Spices
½ teaspoon coriander, ground
½ teaspoon cummin, ground
½ teaspoon chilli powder

SP **Spice pack available**

1 Soak the channa dhal overnight in enough water to cover.
2 Boil the dhal in twice its volume of water until soft, then strain and mash. Add the *spices* and salt.
3 Cook and mash the potatoes in the normal way (about 20 minutes).
4 Shape the potato around the insides of cups of about 2–2½ inches (5–6 cm) in diameter (see drawing). The recipe should give about eight.

5 Fill with a little of the dhal mixture. Enclose in the potato by squeezing, and then flatten to a conventional rissole shape. Roll in breadcrumbs.
6 Fry one side until brown, then turn over and brown the other side.

An alternative way of making the rissoles is to cook 6 oz (175 g) fresh or frozen peas, or 2 fresh, finely chopped chillies, and add them to the mashed potato before shaping.

Makes: about 8

DHAL VADA
Lentil Rissoles

Very much a traditional Indian snack, there are all manner of vadas. For no good reason they rarely appear in restaurants, although, being simple rissole balls, they are easy enough to make.

7 oz (200 g) polished urid dhal

1 teaspoon chopped green
   chillies

salt

vegetable oil for deep-frying

Optional ingredients

2 tablespoons onion, finely
   chopped

2 teaspoons finely chopped
   fresh ginger

6 fresh curry leaves

Spices

½ teaspoon cummin seeds,
   crushed

½ teaspoon black pepper,
   ground

I   Grind the dhal (dry) into flour – use your coffee grinder, small quantities at a time, or a mortar and pestle. Add the chillies, *spices*, salt, and any or all of the *optional ingredients*.

2   Make the mixture into a dough with a little water, and allow to stand for 20 minutes.

3   Roll into ping-pong-ball sized balls. Heat the oil and deep-fry – at a medium heat for 10 minutes, or until golden. Serve hot or cold.

Makes: *about 6–8*

EKOORI

Spiced Scrambled Egg

Egg dishes are less popular in India than in the UK, probably because eggs, like chickens, are less readily available. Parsee Indians, originally from Persia, are especially fond of eggs, and they eat this scrambled egg dish at breakfast, tea or supper. It makes a particularly nice tea-time sandwich filling or toast-topper. The first recipe is the traditional version, the second is much simpler.

1 small onion, finely chopped
¾ inch (2 cm) fresh ginger,
  finely chopped
1 clove garlic, finely chopped
1 green chilli, finely chopped
2 tablespoons ghee
4 eggs
1 small firm tomato, sliced
1 dessertspoon chopped fresh
  coriander or parsley
salt

Spices
⅓ teaspoon black pepper,
  ground
⅓ teaspoon turmeric

1 Fry onion, ginger, garlic and chilli gently in ghee in saucepan for about 10 minutes. Add *spices*, and cook for a further 5 minutes.

2 Break eggs into pan, mix well, and stir and cook until you have the texture required.

3 Add tomato, fresh coriander or parsley and salt about 2 minutes before serving.

Serves: 4

A Simpler Version

1 tablespoon ghee
1 small clove garlic, finely
  chopped (optional)
4 eggs
salt

Spices
⅓ teaspoon white pepper,
  ground
⅓ teaspoon turmeric
⅓ teaspoon fenugreek seeds,
  ground

Melt ghee, add *spices* and garlic, and fry for 1 minute. Add eggs to pan, and salt to taste. Fork up eggs in the pan, and scramble to taste.

INDIAN OMELETTE

Another Parsee favourite, this is a superb recipe which competes well with the Spanish omelette. Serve it with salad or even with chips. It's delicious. The ingredients given are to serve two, but for four or more, increase the filling quantities, but cook the omelette in batches of four eggs at a time. A larger omelette is harder to control.

4 eggs
1 tablespoon ghee
1 tablespoon chopped fresh coriander or parsley

Filling
1 small onion, chopped
1 clove garlic, finely chopped
1 green chilli, chopped
vegetable oil

Spices
⅓ teaspoon turmeric
½ teaspoon coriander, ground
½ teaspoon cummin, ground
½ teaspoon paprika

⅓ red pepper (pimento) in thin strips, blanched
2 boiled potatoes, in ½ inch (12 mm) cubes
salt

1 Make the filling first, by frying the onion, garlic and chilli in some oil until light golden.

2 Add the *spices*, and fry for a further 10 minutes.

3 Add pepper and potato, and fry a further 10–15 minutes. Salt to taste, and set aside. (This can be made in advance.)

4 To make the omelette, heat the ghee and beat eggs with a wire whisk.

5 Pour eggs into pan and cook on low to medium heat until just firm, then turn over.

6 Spread with filling and cook until firm, then fold over the filling. Serve with coriander or parsley as garnish.

Serves: 2

BHEL PURI

Batata Sev Puri

Bhel puri is the snack in Bombay, and you'll find it in pavement stalls and snack bars everywhere. The nearest thing I can liken it to here is popcorn, but it is rather more complicated than that, and certainly heartily recommend that you try it. You'll need to obtain special puffed rice and sev (gram flour strings) from your supplier (all the items marked with an asterisk are available by post from The Curry Club).

Make a larger quantity of the sauce than this if you like – it will keep for weeks in the refrigerator.

1 cup puffed Basmati rice*
½ cup sev*
⅓ cup cocktail puri* (or matti), in small pieces
1 tablespoon raw peanuts*
½ cup diced cold boiled potato
2 tablespoons chopped raw onion
2 green chillies, chopped
2 tablespoons chopped fresh coriander

Sauce
2 inch (5 cm) block tamarind* (see page 16)
1 medium onion, finely chopped
2 cloves garlic, finely chopped
1 tablespoon wine vinegar
1 tablespoon brown sugar
salt

Spices
1 teaspoon paprika
1 teaspoon cummin, ground
1 teaspoon garam masala
½ teaspoon asafoetida
1 dessertspoon dry fenugreek leaves

1 *For the sauce,* boil the tamarind for 10 minutes in 1 cup water. Sieve, and discard husks.

2 Meanwhile, fry onion and garlic until golden, then add the *spices* and fry for a further 5 minutes.

3 Add the tamarind juice, vinegar and sugar, and simmer for 5 minutes. Add more sugar to taste, and salt. The sauce should be fairly runny, so add water as necessary. When cold put it into the food processor or through a sieve to get a thin soup-like consistency.

4 *For the bhel puri,* mix the puffed rice, sev, cocktail puri and peanuts, and put out in serving bowls. Mix the potato, onion, and chillies, and place on top.

5 Serve about 2 tablespoons of sauce on top of that and sprinkle chopped coriander over the lot. Serve cold.

Serves: 4

MATTI or MATHHI
Savoury Biscuits

Mattis are simple to make, and if allowed to cool overnight, they become quite crisp. Store in an airtight tin and they will keep for several weeks – that is, if you've not eaten them first! I've made them round in the recipe, but they can also be cut into strips, triangles or squares.

1 lb (450 g) white flour	**1 dessertspoon salt**
1 dessertspoon ajowan (or cummin) seeds	**4 tablespoons vegetable oil**
	oil for deep-frying

1 Knead the flour, seeds and salt together with the oil. Add enough water to get a very smooth textured dough. Knead for 15–20 minutes. It should be quite stiff.

2 Roll into 1½ inch (3 cm) diameter flat balls, then roll out to a disc 3–3½ inches (8–8 cm) in diameter, and ⅛ inch (3 mm) thick. Make small incisions to prevent them puffing up when frying.

3 Preheat the deep-frying oil to just below smoking point, and fry the biscuits until light gold (not brown), turning as necessary.

4 Allow to cool, then store in an airtight container. Serve on their own, or with chutneys.

Makes: *a small biscuit tin full!*

4
BARBECUES, GRILLS & TANDOORI

Cooking outdoors is one of today's big leisure activities in Europe and particularly in the United States where the enjoyment of leisure is a very serious business indeed. There is a dazzling array of tinny, glossy, painted contraptions on wheels available from consumer-land at anything from £10 upwards on which to cook your food. And if you are a serious barbecuer you will enjoy mastering the tricky process of lighting and controlling your charcoal. But above all you will enjoy the food. Whatever you cook – simple steaks, sausages, potatoes, kebabs – it all tastes so much better over coals.

Our ancestors certainly knew a thing or two: barbecue-style cooking – a luxury perhaps today – was necessity to the ancients. After the discovery of fire, primeval man cooked his food, and, as civilisation developed, so did satisfaction in cooking. By 2000 BC the Greeks had mastered the techniques of kebab cooking and apparatus has been discovered preserved in the lava on the island of Santorini. Now in the national museum in Athens, it consists of pottery walls with indentations of various heights to allow the adjustment of skewers. Cooking took place out of doors – it was easier to control smoke and smells – and the climate was infinitely suitable. There is every reason to believe that this technique was quite common all over the Middle East. It was from there that it spread with the expansion of the

Moslems into the Indian sub-continent.

The Moghuls, perhaps the world's greatest gas-
tronomes, learned to control the techniques to
absolute perfection with the development of their
cylindrical clay oven – the tandoor. This style of
cooking, unique to North-West India (now Pakistan)
and the Punjab is ages old. Curiously, prior to 1947
it was totally unknown elsewhere in the sub-
continent. The partition of India and Pakistan
changed that dramatically. The line on the map that
created the division between the two countries to
satisfy religious differences also brought about re-
settlement of those people on the 'wrong' side of the
line. One of those people was a Hindu restaurateur
who moved down to Delhi to set up a tandoori
restaurant – the first one. Within years the fashion
caught on all over the country, and a decade later it
spread in much the same way all over Britain.

The magic of the tandoor comes from a combination of the style of tandoori food and the oven it is
cooked in. Traditionally there are just four main
tandoori dishes: tandoori chicken, boti kebabs
(lamb), tandoori chupattis and nan bread. Everything
else is new, evolved by modern restaurateurs –
tandoori fish, seafood and tikka are all now cooked
by the tandoor method and they are absolutely
delicious and suited to the process, which involves
an overnight marination of the chicken or meat in
yoghurt and spices. This softens and flavours the
meat, and the distinctive red colouring makes the
food look so appetising on its traditional bed of
lettuce, onion rings and lemon wedges. The nan
bread also contains yoghurt, and is shaped by hand
rather than by rolling pin.

The tandoor itself is a clay oven which perfectly
complements the raw food by giving it a unique
flavour during cooking. It is about 5 feet (1.5 m) deep
and 2 feet (60 cm) in diameter at the base. It curves
in at the top end to a hole about 1 foot (30 cm) in
diameter, and it resembles the shape of a bullet.
Normally they are sited out of doors and below the
ground. Charcoal is lit in the bottom of the oven 2 or
3 hours before cooking begins, allowing enough time
to heat the base of the oven to red hot. The chefs sit
on the ground in front of the opening and place the
meat or chicken on a very long sharp skewer. The tip
sits on the charcoal and the meat about 1–1½ feet
(30–45 cm) up the skewer. It cooks for about 20–25
minutes and is taken out two or three times for

A TANDOOR (CLAY OVEN)

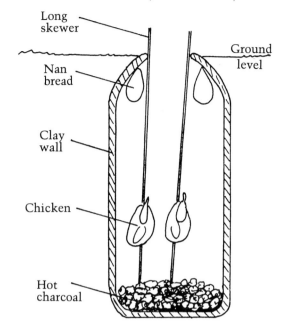

Long
skewer

Ground
level

Nan
bread

Clay
wall

Chicken

Hot
charcoal

basting with marinade and ghee. Nans are literally slapped onto the inside top of the oven where the dough adheres to the clay and the nan adopts its traditional teardrop shape. Outside a busy city restaurant in India there may be as many as six or eight tandoors. One useful service, not to be found in the UK, is the tandoor walla – the oven man or baker – who will, for a few pennies, bake the food of his clients – a kind of 'take *to*' service! On the market now are small indoor tandoors as used by most restaurants. There are portables for use at outdoor events like fairs, and there is even a stainless steel 'tandoor' for operation on modern gas stoves available all over India.

It is not necessary for you to sink a tandoor in your back garden, although you would get the best flavours from your cooking. An ordinary shop-bought barbecue using charcoal makes a very close substitute, or you can make your own simple, effective, cheap barbecue. Failing all that you can still get good results using your oven and grill. Have a go ... you'll be surprised how easy it is.

TANDOORI CHICKEN
(or Turkey, Duck, Quails, Pigeon etc)

Nearly every Indian restaurant offers tandoori dishes, whether or not they own a tandoor. The dish needs no introduction although the method probably does. The tasty secret lies in a long marinade in yoghurt with spices. The colouring used to be achieved by using alkenet root but is more simply obtained now by using red, yellow or orange food colouring powder. You can choose your own colour. Although you do get a better flavour using charcoal, the results under the grill are totally satisfactory.

3 lb (1.4 kg) chicken or 4 large
  legs
3 tablespoons lime or lemon
  juice
1 teaspoon salt

Marinade
6 fl oz (175 ml) yoghurt
2 tablespoons mustard oil
6 cloves garlic
1 teaspoon salt

Marinade spices
1½ teaspoons paprika
1½ teaspoons coriander,
  ground
1½ teaspoons cummin,
  ground
1 teaspoon ground ginger
¼ teaspoon orange food
  colouring powder
SP *Spice pack available*

1 Skin the chicken, then quarter it and slash the flesh with short gashes. Rub in the lime or lemon juice and the salt. Leave for half an hour or so.

2 Meanwhile mix all the marinade ingredients, including the *spices*, either in a blender or by hand. Rub it thoroughly into the chicken (by hand is messy but best), and leave to stand in a bowl overnight (covered, to minimise smells).

3 Next day preheat the oven to 425°F (220°C) Gas 7. Shake excess marinade off chicken pieces and place on oven racks. Make sure to put a drip pan underneath.

4 Cook for 25–30 minutes, then, to finish off, place under grill for 3–4 minutes.

5 Alternatively, if you are barbecuing, put the pieces of marinated chicken over the charcoal (not too near) and cook until ready.

6 Serve on a bed of lettuce and onion rings with a wedge of lemon, and some nan bread and tandoori chutney (see pages 130 and 143).

Serves: 4

TANDOORI FISH

(or Lobster, Crayfish, Scampi, King Prawns etc)

Not traditional to the tandoor process – fish was hard to come by in the Punjab – but it works very well, and has recently become an Indian delicacy. The choice of fish is up to you: mackerel, trout and salmon are all excellent, but most fish and shellfish will do.

about 2 lb (900 g) filleted fish
2 tablespoons lime or lemon
   juice
1 teaspoon salt

Marinade and marinade
   spices
**as for Tandoori Chicken, but
   with less garlic (about 2–3
   cloves)**

I Lightly slash the fillets with the sharp point of a knife then pour on the lime or lemon juice and salt. Stand for 15 minutes.

2 Make the marinade as for Tandoori Chicken, and pour it onto the fish, ensuring both sides are covered. Leave to marinate for at least 6 hours, preferably overnight, covered, in the refrigerator.

3 Preheat the oven to 375°F (190°C) Gas 5. Place the fish on foil on wire racks (with a drip pan underneath) and cook for 20 minutes or so. Keep a close eye on the fish all the time as it may need slightly less or more cooking.

4 Alternatively, cook over barbecue until ready (about 10–15 minutes, depending on heat and thickness of fish).

5 Serve and garnish as Tandoori Chicken.

Serves: 4

×MAKHANWALLA
Tandoori Chicken Curry

Rapidly becoming a restaurant favourite and rightly so. It can also be called Tandoori Chicken Makhani or Masalador.

4 chicken legs and 4 breast
  pieces
2 tablespoons lemon juice
6 fl oz (175 ml) yoghurt
1 medium onion, roughly
  chopped
2 cloves garlic, roughly
  chopped
2 inch (5 cm) fresh ginger,
  roughly chopped
½ cup vegetable oil
2 tomatoes, chopped
1 dessertspoon tomato purée
2 tablespoons chopped fresh
  coriander
salt

Spices 1 (Marinade)
1½ teaspoons paprika
1½ teaspoons coriander,
  ground
1½ teaspoons cummin,
  ground
1 teaspoon ground ginger
¼ teaspoon orange food
  colouring powder

Spices 2
½ teaspoon mustard seeds
½ teaspoon cummin seeds

Spices 3
2 teaspoons paprika
1 teaspoon garam masala
1 teaspoon coriander, ground
¼ teaspoon yellow food
  colouring powder
1 teaspoon garlic powder

SP *Spice pack available*

1 Skin the chicken, lightly prick or gash the flesh, and rub in the lemon juice. Leave for 10 minutes.

2 Make the marinade by combining the yoghurt and *spices 1*. Pour over the chicken, and mix well. Leave for 24 hours if possible (refrigerated), or for a minimum of 6 hours.

3 The next day, preheat the oven to 300°F (150°C) Gas 2. Remove the chicken from the marinade, ensuring that there is a liberal coating left on each piece. Place on oven tray and bake for 20 minutes, then remove. Strain liquid off oven tray and reserve.

4 Meanwhile, purée the onion, garlic and ginger together in a processor or blender.

5 Heat the oil in a pan and fry *spices 2* until they pop (about 2 minutes). Add the onion/garlic/ginger purée and *spices 3* to the pan, and simmer for some 10 minutes.

6 Add the tomatoes, tomato purée, spare yoghurt marinade, and the cooking liquid (see 3 above), and simmer for a while. Add the cooked chicken, coriander and salt. Simmer for a further 10–15 minutes, then serve.

Serves: 4

TIKKA

(Lobster, Turkey, Chicken or Lamb)

This is a great favourite. The real way to cook it is in a tandoor, but it is almost as good over charcoal. You can also use the grill.

1½ lb (675 g) meat
8 oz (225 g) onion, coarsely chopped
3 oz (75 g) tomato purée
salt to taste

Spices
½ teaspoon black pepper, ground
1 teaspoon white cummin, ground
½ teaspoon ground ginger
½ teaspoon mango powder
¼ teaspoon red food colouring powder

SP *Spice pack available*

1 Discard any fat, skin or shell, then cube the meat.
2 Make a purée in the blender of onion, tomato purée, salt and *spices* – add a little water to help them blend together.
3 Put the meat cubes into the purée and marinate overnight, or for a minimum of 4 hours.
4 Put meat onto skewers and cook over charcoal grill. Or cover the grill-pan rack with foil, then place the individual tikkas on the foil and grill at a medium heat. Cook both ways for about 10–15 minutes.
5 Serve with a green salad, onion rings, lemon wedges, nan bread and tandoori chutney (see pages 130 and 143).

Serves: 4

TANDOORI MURGH HARIALI
Green Tandoori

Chicken marinated in spinach and fresh herbs. An unusual tandoori dish.

2 small chickens or poussins
(about 2 lb or 900 g each)
2 tablespoons lemon juice
2 inch (5 cm) fresh ginger
3 cloves garlic
8 oz (225 g) spring onions
2¼ lb (1 kg) fresh coriander
leaves

8 oz (225 g) fresh mint leaves
1 lb (450 g) spinach, washed
and prepared
8 green chillies
16 fl oz (400 ml) yoghurt
salt and pepper to taste
1 cup mustard oil

Spices
1 tablespoon garam masala

1 Skin the chickens, slit the breasts and legs, and remove all the fat. Marinate in lemon juice for a minimum of 4 hours.

2 Grind together (by hand or in a blender) the ginger, garlic, spring onions, coriander and mint leaves, spinach and green chillies. When ground finely, add to the yoghurt, then mix in the *spice*, salt, pepper and mustard oil.

3 Rub thoroughly onto the chicken (best by hand) and leave to stand in bowl overnight (covered in refrigerator).

4 The next day, preheat the oven to 400°F (200°C) Gas 6, and shake excess marinade off chickens. Place on oven racks (with drip pan underneath) and cook for 25–30 minutes.

5 Alternatively, if barbecuing, joint before placing over the heat, then cook until ready.

6 When cooked, separate the legs from the breast, then serve on a bed of lettuce and onion rings with a wedge of lemon, with nan bread and tandoori chutney (see pages 130 and 143).

Serves: 4–6

KEBABS

Seekh (Stick or Skewer) and Shami (Balls)

These are great at barbecues, and as a snack, starter or main course, and are familiar friends at the Indian restaurant. You should get about eight kebabs from this mix. Serve with salad, lemon wedges and tandoori chutney (page 143).

1 oz (25 g) channa dhal, split
8 oz (225 g) fatless stewing
  steak
½ large onion, chopped
1 inch (2.5 cm) fresh ginger,
  chopped
1 large clove garlic, chopped
salt to taste
ghee or oil
1 egg yolk
¼ cup chopped fresh
  coriander or parsley
fine breadcrumbs

Spices
1 brown cardamom, ground
1 bay leaf
¼ teaspoon black pepper,
  ground
½ teaspoon paprika
½ teaspoon garam masala

SP *Spice pack available*

I Soak the dhal overnight, then boil in twice its volume of water. Strain off any excess water.

2 Put the meat, onion, ginger, garlic and *spices* through a mincer. Mix well and add salt to taste.

3 Add the dhal to the mixture, and fry in a little ghee for 20 minutes. Add a *little* water if it dries up too much. Leave aside for about 3 hours or overnight to thicken and dry.

4 The next day, or when ready, add the egg yolk, and, if it doesn't hold together, add gram flour to thicken or water to thin. Add fresh coriander or parsley.

5 For *Seekh Kebabs* roll mixture in breadcrumbs to sausage shapes. Skewer them and cook over charcoal (best), under the grill or fry in a frying pan.

6 For *Shami Kebabs*, roll into balls, coat in breadcrumbs and deep-fry.

Makes: *about 8*

KEBABS
An alternative method

This is a totally different way to make kebabs. The meat is raw and no dhal is used. The secret here is to 'purée' the meat yourself (minced meat will not bind), and to use skewers to maintain the shape.

1 lb (450 g) best lean lamb or
    beef steak
1 teaspoon salt

Spices
1 teaspoon cummin, ground
1 teaspoon black pepper,
    ground
1 tablespoon fenugreek
    leaves, dry
1½ teaspoons garlic powder
1 teaspoon cornflour

1 Remove any fat or unwanted parts from the meat.

2 Chop the meat into chunks, then put it and the *spices* into a food processor to obtain an even purée. (You can do the same by hand pounding, and hard work it is too!) Do not add any water whatever you do – it will cause the kebabs to break up while cooking.

3 Shape the purée onto 4 or 8 skewers (or into sausage shapes if you do not have skewers).

4 Cook them under the grill, or on a barbecue, for about 10 minutes.

Serves: *4 large or 8 small kebabs*

BOTI KEBAB

Boti is a lamb kebab marinated in yoghurt and skewered, then well cooked in the tandoor. Beef, pork or veal can also be used.

If you intend to serve any of these kebabs as a starter for 4 people, then 1½ lb (675 g) is too much meat. Buy half quantities, but remember to also halve the marinade spice quantities given for Tandoori Chicken (page 58).

1½ lb (675 g) lamb in 1 inch
(2.5 cm) cubes
2 tablespoons lemon or lime
juice
1 teaspoon salt

*Marinade and marinade
spices*
as for Tandoori Chicken (see
page 58) plus 1 tablespoon
tomato purée

1 Trim fat off meat (although if you like it well cooked in the barbecue, leave it on), then prick cubes with a sharp pointed knife. Pour on the lemon or lime juice and salt and stand for 30 minutes.

2 Meanwhile make the marinade, and add the tomato purée. Pour over the meat, mix thoroughly, and leave to stand overnight.

3 The next day, preheat the grill to medium-hot, and put the meat onto skewers.

4 Cook until ready (about 10–15 minutes), adjusting heat as necessary. Alternatively, barbecue the meat. Serve as other tandoori dishes.

Serves: 4

GURDA KEBAB

These are lamb's kidneys which are marinated in yoghurt, skewered and grilled or barbecued as above. Use 1½ lb (675 g) kidneys in place of meat. All other ingredients as for Boti Kebab.

KALEJI KEBAB

As Boti Kebab, but use 1½ lb (675 lb) lamb's liver instead of the meat.

CHAAMP
Lamb Chop

Simple to prepare, incredible to taste, and ideal for the barbecue or grill. (You could use pork or mutton chops instead, if you like.)

8 lamb chops, about 4 oz
  (115 g) each
salt
4 cloves garlic, crushed
1 inch (2.5 cm) fresh ginger
1 cup yoghurt

Spices
2 teaspoons garam masala
1 teaspoon paprika
1/8 teaspoon red food
  colouring powder (optional)
1/2 teaspoon chilli powder
  (optional)

1 Prick the chops with a fork, and sprinkle salt on them. Leave for a few minutes.
2 Make a purée of the garlic, ginger, yoghurt and *spices*.
3 Rub the marinade onto the chops and leave for 24 hours maximum, 12 hours minimum.
4 Cook under the grill or over charcoal, for 10–20 minutes, depending on size and thickness of chops.

***Serves:* 4**

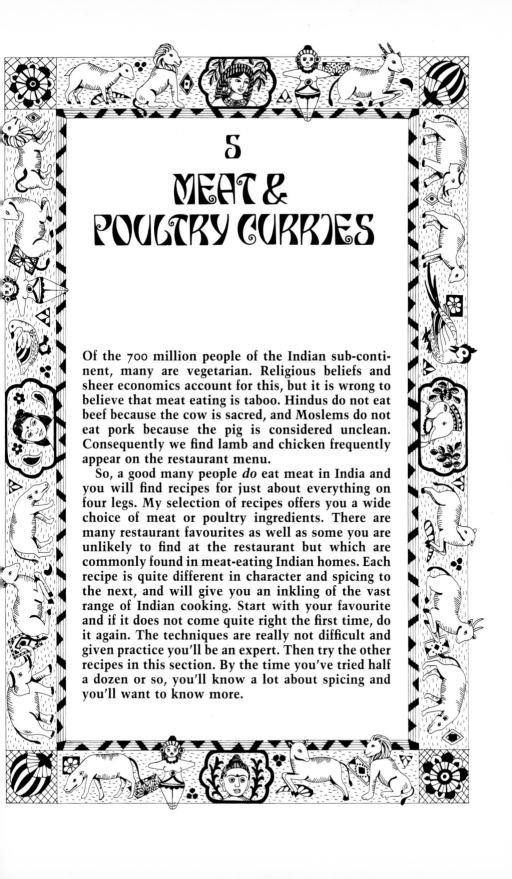

5
MEAT &
POULTRY CURRIES

Of the 700 million people of the Indian sub-continent, many are vegetarian. Religious beliefs and sheer economics account for this, but it is wrong to believe that meat eating is taboo. Hindus do not eat beef because the cow is sacred, and Moslems do not eat pork because the pig is considered unclean. Consequently we find lamb and chicken frequently appear on the restaurant menu.

So, a good many people *do* eat meat in India and you will find recipes for just about everything on four legs. My selection of recipes offers you a wide choice of meat or poultry ingredients. There are many restaurant favourites as well as some you are unlikely to find at the restaurant but which are commonly found in meat-eating Indian homes. Each recipe is quite different in character and spicing to the next, and will give you an inkling of the vast range of Indian cooking. Start with your favourite and if it does not come quite right the first time, do it again. The techniques are really not difficult and given practice you'll be an expert. Then try the other recipes in this section. By the time you've tried half a dozen or so, you'll know a lot about spicing and you'll want to know more.

BEEF CHILLI FRY

The beauty of this recipe is that you can make it as hot as you like. This recipe has been in my family for as long as I can remember. I don't know whether it is authentic, but it is simple to make and deliciously different. Serve with kedgeree (page 130) and/or roti (page 132).

1½ lb (675 g) frying steak
2 large onions, very finely chopped
4 cloves garlic, very finely chopped
2 inch (5 cm) fresh ginger, finely chopped
ghee or oil
6 fresh green chillies
14 oz (400 g) tin tomatoes, strained
salt

Spices
1½ teaspoons coriander seeds, roasted and ground
1 teaspoon cummin seeds, roasted and ground
¼ teaspoon fennel seeds, roasted and ground
pinch fenugreek seeds
2 cloves
1 green cardamom
2 teaspoons paprika
1 teaspoon chilli powder (optional – more if you like!)

SP **Spice pack available**

I Trim the steak of any fat, and chop in 2 inch (5 cm) pieces.

2 Fry the onion, garlic and ginger in the ghee or oil until golden. Add the green chillies (chopped if you like) and cook until soft.

3 Add the *spices*, mix in well, and cook for 5 minutes. Add the tomatoes, mash them in the pan, and cook for 5 minutes.

4 Add the meat. Either cook in the pan on top of the stove, or braise in the oven at 375°F (190°C) Gas 5, for 30–45 minutes. Add some of the juice from the tomatoes if it gets too dry. The meat should be tender in a nice rich sauce. Salt to taste before serving.

Serves: 4

PASANDA
Sliced Beef Curry

This dish is well known in the Indian restaurant. It is based on a traditional Moslem dish which originated in the courts of the emperors centuries ago. Beef was the meat used then, although lamb has become better known. The difference with this dish is that the meat is in slices. I have used beef marinated in red wine (a restaurant technique), and the resultant curry is exceptionally nice.

4 × 8 oz (225 g) pieces steak (fillet, sirloin, rump etc, according to your pocket)
½ pint (300 ml) red wine
1 large onion, roughly chopped
4 cloves garlic, roughly chopped
2 inch (5 cm) fresh ginger, roughly chopped
½ cup oil
2 tablespoons ground almonds
20 whole almonds
1 tablespoon tomato purée
salt

Spices 1
1 teaspoon turmeric
1 teaspoon cummin, ground
1 teaspoon coriander, ground
1 teaspoon paprika
1 teaspoon chilli powder
1 teaspoon poppy seeds

Spices 2
1 tablespoon dry fenugreek leaves
1 dessertspoon garam masala

SP *Spice pack available*

1 Beat the steak out to thin pieces less than ¼ inch (6 mm) thick with a wooden meat hammer. This is called the 'pasanda'. Place meat in a flat bowl, cover with the wine, and leave overnight.

2 Fry the onion, garlic and ginger in some oil until golden. Cool, then purée.

3 Fry the purée in remaining oil and, when simmering, add *spices 1*. Fry at quite a high temperature for about 5 minutes, and keep stirring. Mix in the ground and whole almonds, the tomato purée and a little water if it is too dry.

4 Combine the meat, wine marinade and purée mixture in a shallow casserole dish, ensuring the meat is well covered, salt to taste and cook for 35–40 minutes in a preheated oven at 375°F (190°C) Gas 5.

5 Meanwhile soak *spices 2* in water. After 35–40 minutes, add to the casserole and stir in well. Cook on for a further 20 minutes, then serve. If at any stage it looks too dry, add a little water.

Serves: *4*

KOFTA

Meatball Curry

Koftas are a central Indian speciality. Serve with plain rice and/or chupattis.

1½ lb (675 g) lean stewing
   steak
1 large clove garlic, finely
   chopped
1 egg yolk
½ cup chopped fresh parsley
oil for deep-frying

Sauce
2 tablespoons ghee or corn oil
1 large onion, chopped
14 oz (400 g) tin tomatoes
salt

Spices 1
1 teaspoon coriander, ground
½ teaspoon mango powder
¼ teaspoon chilli powder
2 teaspoons cummin seeds
1 dessertspoon gram flour

Spices 2
1 teaspoon paprika
1 teaspoon turmeric
¼ teaspoon asafoetida
1 dessertspoon garam masala
1 dessertspoon dry fenugreek
   leaves

SP *Spice pack available*

1 To make the meatballs, put the meat, garlic, egg yolk, parsley and *spices 1* through a mincer.

2 Mix well, then form into 1½ inch (3–4 cm) balls – you'll get about 24. Stand them on one side for 3 hours (or overnight) to dry out.

3 Preheat deep-frying oil to hot. Fry balls for 2 minutes each. Put aside.

4 To make the sauce, heat ghee and fry onion. When golden, add *spices 2*. Mix and cook 1 minute then add tomatoes. Add a cup of water (or stock or any soup) and simmer for 10 minutes or so. Salt to taste.

5 The sauce should not be too thick nor too runny (thicken with rice flour, or thin with water as required). Keep simmering, then add the meatballs. Simmer for a further 30 minutes, but avoid vigorous stirring or you might break the balls up.

Serves: 4–6

Keema

Mince Curry with Hard-boiled Eggs

A simple, relatively cheap dish which is very tasty and freezes well (without the egg garnish). Serve with dhal and parathas (see pages 120 and 134). You could use beef, veal, lamb or pork, and you can either get your butcher to mince it for you, or you can do it yourself at home.

1½ lb (675 g) lean meat
1 large onion, finely chopped
2 cloves garlic, finely chopped
2 inch (5 cm) fresh ginger, finely chopped
2 tablespoons ghee
14 oz (400 g) tin tomatoes
1 dessertspoon tomato ketchup
8 oz (225 g) tin tomato soup
salt
2 eggs, hard-boiled, sliced

Spices 1
1 teaspoon turmeric
1 teaspoon coriander, ground
½ teaspoon chilli powder
4 cloves
1 brown cardamom

Spices 2
1 dessertspoon garam masala
1 tablespoon dry fenugreek leaves

SP *Spice pack available*

1 Cut any fat or sinews from the meat, and mince it finely.

2 Fry onion, garlic and ginger over a medium heat in the ghee until golden. Add *spices 1* and simmer for 10 more minutes or so. Add a little water if it dries up too much.

3 Mix the mince, tomatoes and ketchup into the onion mixture, then transfer to a casserole dish. Put into preheated oven at 400°F (200°C) Gas 6, and cook for 40 minutes. Check it half-way through cooking time, stirring if it sticks.

4 Add the tomato soup and *spices 2*. Continue to cook in the oven for a further half hour. Salt to taste.

5 Hard-boil the eggs and slice. Put slices onto the curry to garnish as you serve.

Serves: 4

DAHI WALA
Beef Curry

This is a spicy, creamy curry, made with beef or lamb plus yoghurt, and it goes well with plain rice and/or chupattis.

1½ lb (675 g) lean lamb or beef
½ lb (225 g) onions, coarsely chopped
2 cloves garlic, chopped
1 inch (2.5 cm) fresh ginger, chopped
4 oz (115 g) tin tomatoes
8 fl oz (225 ml) plain yoghurt
4 tablespoons ghee
1 dessertspoon chopped fresh coriander or parsley
salt

Spices 1
1 bay leaf
2 brown cardamoms
3 cloves
2 inch (5 cm) cassia bark

Spices 2
½ teaspoon turmeric
¼ teaspoon black pepper, ground
1 teaspoon coriander, ground
1 teaspoon cummin, ground
½ teaspoon chilli powder

Spices 3
1 dessertspoon dry fenugreek leaves
1 dessertspoon garam masala

SP *Spice pack available*

1 Trim the meat of any fat, and cut into 1 inch (2.5 cm) cubes.

2 Put onions, garlic, ginger, tomatoes and yoghurt into blender, and purée. Mix the meat and the blend in a bowl with *spices 1*. Marinate overnight, or for a minimum of 6 hours.

3 Heat ghee to medium, and add the blend and marinated meat. Stir frequently. When paste starts changing colour, add *spices 2*. If this gets dry while you are cooking, add a *little* water. Cook for 20 minutes or so.

4 Add *spices 3* plus the fresh coriander or parsley and cook for a further 20 minutes – or more (it does not matter if you cook for longer, it's up to you: the flavour changes the longer you cook it. You can also leave it to marinate after cooking for a further day prior to serving). Salt to taste.

Serves: 4

RHOGAN JOSH GOSHT
Lamb in Red Gravy

This is one of the traditional dishes from the times of the Moghul emperors. In ancient days they used alkenet root to redden the meat, but in this recipe I have used tomato, paprika and red food colouring. The flavour is fantastic and I have used an authentic Kashmiri recipe rather than a simplified restaurateur's version. Serve with pullao rice (page 123).

1½ lb (675 g) lean lamb, cubed
4 fl oz (115 ml) yoghurt
salt
½ lb (225 g) onion, roughly
  chopped
2 inch (5 cm) fresh ginger,
  roughly chopped
2 cloves garlic
14 oz (400 g) tin tomatoes (or
  fresh)
about 8 dessertspoons ghee
1 tablespoon chopped fresh
  coriander

Spices 1
3 green cardamoms
3 cloves
3 small pieces cassia bark
½ teaspoon turmeric
½ teaspoon chilli powder
1 teaspoon coriander, ground
1 teaspoon cummin, ground

Spices 2
1 dessertspoon garam masala
2 teaspoons paprika
⅛ teaspoon red food
  colouring powder

1 Mix the lamb and yoghurt, *spices 1* and salt. Let stand for 6 hours minimum or overnight.

2 Put onion, ginger, garlic and tomato into blender, and purée.

3 Melt ghee in a pan, and add the onion purée. Put the lamb mixture into a separate pan (without ghee). Cook both for about 20–30 minutes. Salt to taste, and stir the meat occasionally to prevent sticking.

4 Combine the two mixtures and cook for a further half hour or so, until the meat is quite tender.

5 Add *spices 2*, and fresh coriander. Mix well and cook for a further 5 minutes, then serve.

If at any time the curry gets too dry, add a little water. Alternatively, after both meat and purée have been fried, they can be put in a casserole dish in the oven preheated to 375°F (190°C) Gas 5 and baked for 45 minutes. Add *spices 2* and cook for a further 10–15 minutes. Add fresh coriander and serve.

Serves: *4*

SAAG or SAG GOSHT
Lamb in Puréed Spinach

A recipe beloved by families all over India, this is lamb prepared in spinach, ginger and garlic. It is savoury, tasty, delicious, and also very nutritious!

As an alternative to spinach you can use sarson-ka-sag (mustard leaves). Use about 6 oz (175 g) out of a tin (available from The Curry Club) or 4 oz (115 g) plus ½ lb (225 g) fresh spinach.

1½ lb (675 g) lean lamb
1 large onion, finely chopped
ghee or oil
2 inch (5 cm) fresh ginger, finely chopped
2 cloves garlic, finely chopped
4 fresh tomatoes, chopped
1 lb (450 g) spinach, washed and chopped
4 tablespoons chopped fresh coriander
salt

Spices 1
4 cloves
2 brown cardamoms
1 teaspoon cummin seeds

Spices 2
½ teaspoon turmeric
½ teaspoon chilli powder
½ teaspoon black pepper, ground
½ teaspoon coriander, ground

Spices 3
1 teaspoon garam masala
1 dessertspoon dry fenugreek leaves

I Remove any fat, and cut meat into cubes.

2 Fry the onion until golden in some ghee or oil, then add the ginger, garlic and *spices 1*. Add the tomatoes after 5 minutes.

3 At the same time seal the meat by lightly browning in a separate saucepan. Stir to prevent sticking.

4 Combine the two, and add *spices 2* and the spinach. Stir it all about to ensure it does not stick. If it seems too dry (and this depends on the meat) add a little water.

5 Simmer until the meat is tender – about 45–60 minutes – then add *spices 3* and fresh coriander and cook on for at least 10 minutes. Salt to taste.

As with most meat curries you can serve at once or leave overnight or freeze. The taste will alter slightly in each case but all are delicious!

Serves: *4*

MUTTON XACUTTI

This dish, pronounced 'Zacewtee' is a Goanese speciality. Goa, some 400 miles south of Bombay on India's west coast, is a sheer heaven of palm trees and golden beaches that used to be a Portuguese colony. Its cuisine is quite unique, and this dish is typical – a recipe used by the chefs at the Hotel Cicade de Goa, one of the top local hotels.

**2 lb (900 g) lean lamb or
    mutton**
2 tablespoons ghee or oil
juice of 1 lemon
salt

Spices 1
3 teaspoons coriander seeds
8 whole dried red chillies
½ teaspoon fenugreek seeds
5 black peppercorns
4 green cardamoms
6 cloves
1 inch (2.5 cm) cassia bark
½ teaspoon cummin seeds
1 tablespoon raw peanuts

Spices 2
1 teaspoon turmeric
**1 tablespoon fresh grated or
    desiccated coconut**

1 Remove any fat, and cut meat into cubes.

2 Roast *spices 1* in a dry pan on top of the stove, until the cummin seeds change to brown. Smell that aroma! Cool, then grind finely in coffee grinder or mortar. Add *spices 2*.

3 Warm the ghee or oil, add the spices and cook gently for 5 minutes. Add meat, and stir until water has dried out of meat and it is well browned.

4 Add 4 fl oz (115 ml) water and simmer until meat is tender (about 45 minutes).

5 Add lemon juice and salt a few minutes before cooking is complete. Serve with plain rice. Squeeze more lemon juice on to taste.

Serves: 4

SORPORTEL

Pork Curry

This is a remarkable dish which also comes from Goa – where they have no taboos concerning meats or other ingredients – and uses pork meat, liver and heart.

1 lb (450 g) lean pork, off the bone
1 pig's liver
1 pig's heart
1 large onion, roughly chopped
8 cloves garlic, roughly chopped
2 inch (5 cm) fresh ginger
6 fresh chillies
1 cup oil
1 cup vinegar
salt to taste

Spices
1 teaspoon cummin seeds
1 inch (2.5 cm) cassia bark
6 cloves
1 teaspoon turmeric
2 teaspoons black peppercorns
2 teaspoons paprika
½ teaspoon asafoetida

1 Clean and chop the three meats into 1½ inch (3–4 cm) cubes.

2 Boil about 2 cups water, add the cubed meat, and simmer until tender (about 15 minutes). Strain and reserve liquid.

3 Meanwhile purée the onion, garlic, ginger and chillies.

4 Heat the oil and fry the purée until the oil floats (about 10–15 minutes), then add the *spices*. Fry for a further 5 minutes, keeping it hot and stirring continuously.

5 Add the meat to the purée with the vinegar and salt, and cook on for a further 20–30 minutes.

This dish is much better if allowed to marinate for at least a day after cooking. It is even better after several days. Keep it in the refrigerator until you wish to serve it (or freeze, of course).

Serves: 4

DHANSAK

Chicken in Lentil Purée

The Parsees who, centuries ago, were refugees from Persia, now live on India's west coast. Much of their cooking is very distinctive, and Dhansak is probably their most famous and delicious dish, now established as something very special all over India. Dhansak means wealthy, and when you try this recipe (which tastes very much better than most restaurant dhansaks) you'll know why – it's a real treat!

You can use capon, turkey, lamb, beef or veal instead of the chicken, and if you do not have all the types of lentils, use any type. Serve with parathas (page 134).and/or rice.

1 oz (25 g) each channa, moong and red dhal

2 oz (50 g) toor dhal

½ cup corn or sunflower oil

1½ lb (675 g) poultry (off the bone) or meat in 1 inch (2.5 cm) cubes

3 medium onions, finely chopped

2 cloves garlic, finely chopped

salt

14 oz (400 g) tin tomatoes

1 small/medium aubergine, chopped

1 large potato, peeled and chopped

4 oz (115 g) fresh, frozen or tinned spinach

½ cup chopped fresh coriander

¼ cup chopped fresh mint

Spices 1

1 teaspoon cummin seeds

1 brown cardamom

2 inch (5 cm) cassia bark

½ teaspoon black mustard seeds

Spices 2

1 teaspoon turmeric

1 teaspoon coriander, ground

1 teaspoon cummin, ground

¼ teaspoon fenugreek seeds, ground

½ teaspoon chilli powder

SP *Spice pack available*

1 Wash the lentils, searching for grit etc. Soak overnight.

2 The next day, cook lentils in twice their volume of water for 30 minutes.

3 Meanwhile, heat the oil and fry meat at high temperature for 5–10 minutes. Remove meat from pan and keep warm.

4 Fry *spices 1* in fat and juices in the pan, adding onions and garlic and salt. When golden, add tomatoes, and fry for a further 5 minutes.

5 Add remaining chopped vegetables and cook for about 10 minutes.

6 Add the lentils and coarsely mash the lot inside the pan. Add the meat and *spices 2*. Cook on for about 40 minutes. Add fresh herbs (if you have them) and cook a further 10 minutes minimum.

Serves: *4 or more*

MURGH MASALA
Spiced Whole Roast Chicken

You will often find this on the Indian restaurant menu (also called Kurzi Chicken), described as requiring 24 hours' notice to make. This is because a whole chicken must be marinated for at least 6 hours before being cooked – not the sort of thing a restaurant can do on spec! Murgh means chicken in Hindi, and masala, as we all know, means spice mixture. The chicken should be fairly dry and crusty, and should taste spicy and tangy. It is quite superb.

3–3½ lb (1.4–1.5 kg) roasting chicken

1 large onion, coarsely chopped

2 inch (5 cm) fresh ginger, coarsely chopped

4 fl oz (115 ml) yoghurt

1 tablespoon fresh lemon or lime juice

salt

4 tablespoons ghee or corn oil

2 cloves garlic, finely chopped

½ cup chopped fresh coriander or parsley

1 tomato, thinly sliced

Spices 1

2 bay leaves

1 brown cardamom

2 cloves

4 peppercorns

Spices 2

½ teaspoon chilli powder

1 teaspoon coriander, ground

½ teaspoon black cummin seeds

½ teaspoon turmeric

Stuffing

½ cup Basmati rice, par-boiled

2 tablespoons frozen peas

1 tablespoon prawns

SP *Spice pack available*

1 Skin the chicken, keeping it whole, and gash the flesh a little. Rub all over, inside and outside, with a blend (puréed or hand-mixed) of the onion, ginger, yoghurt, lemon or lime juice and a little salt. Put in a bowl and marinate overnight (a minimum of 6 hours).

2 Remove the chicken from the blend and fry in the ghee or oil, turning carefully until all sides are browned (about 15 minutes). Remove from the pan, leaving the ghee and blend behind. When the chicken is cold enough, stuff with the stuffing mixture plus *spices 1*.

3 Fry the garlic in the pan, add *spices 2*, any remaining blend, and salt to taste, and simmer gently. Add ¼ pint (150 ml) water bit by bit over 10 minutes.

4 Put the chicken on its back in a large lidded casserole dish and pour the fried blend over it. Put the lid on and place into preheated oven at 400°F (200°C) Gas 6. Cook for about an hour, basting once or twice.

5 Sprinkle the fresh coriander or parsley over chicken, and put the tomato slices on top. Cook without the lid for a minimum of 10 minutes. You'll probably need longer, and possibly an increase in heat to crust and dry the chicken, it's up to you. Keep a close eye on it. Sieve off any spare oil (keep for future use) and serve the blend 'gravy' over the chicken.

Serves: 4

GOAN VINEGAR CHICKEN

This is another unique Goan dish. You can substitute pork or veal for the chicken if you prefer.

3–3½ lb (1.4–1.5 kg) chicken
2 large onions, chopped
3–4 tablespoons vegetable oil
4 cloves garlic, finely chopped
2 inch (5 cm) fresh ginger,
  finely chopped
1 cup vinegar
4 fresh green chillies, chopped
  (optional)
salt

Spices
½ teaspoon coriander, ground
½ teaspoon cloves, ground
½ teaspoon cassia bark,
  ground
½ teaspoon turmeric
½ teaspoon chilli powder

1 Joint the chicken into 8 pieces.

2 Fry the onions in some of the oil for about 5 minutes, then add the garlic and ginger and simmer for another 10–15 minutes.

3 Mix the *spices* with water to make a paste. Add to the onions etc and fry on for 10 more minutes or so. Add a little water if it gets too dry. Keep stirring.

4 Meanwhile fry the chicken pieces in a separate pan in remaining oil, until the pieces are browned (about 10 minutes).

5 Place the onion mixture and the chicken into a casserole dish, add the vinegar, chillies (if using), salt and a little water and cook in a preheated oven at 350°F (180°C) Gas 4 for 45 minutes (or until the chicken is tender).

Serves: 4

BHOONA
Dry Fried Curry

Bhoona or bhuna, which means fried in Hindustani, is a traditional type of curry. In many restaurants it appears as a dry mild curry in a rich creamy coconut sauce. This recipe is based on a traditional Indian style. You can use any type of meat – lamb, beef, pork, chicken etc.

1½ lb (675 g) lean meat
2 tablespoons ghee or
   vegetable oil
6–8 oz (175–225 g) onions,
   roughly chopped
2 cloves garlic
2 medium tomatoes
1 tablespoon vinegar
2 oz (50 g) creamed coconut
   (or desiccated equivalent)
salt to taste

Spices
1 teaspoon garam masala
1 teaspoon coriander, ground
½ teaspoon chilli powder
½ teaspoon turmeric

SP *Spice pack available*

1   Cut any fat off the meat and cut into cubes. Heat most of the oil or ghee and fry meat for 5–10 minutes.

2   Pound in a mortar and pestle, or blend or liquidise the onions, garlic, tomatoes and vinegar.

3   Put this mixture in a separate pan with remaining ghee, add *spices*, and stir-fry for 5 minutes.

4   Combine meat, coconut and fried blend. Simmer until meat is tender. It should be quite dry with little gravy, but stir frequently, adding a little water if it sticks. Salt to taste.

   Alternatively, casserole in oven at 375°F (190°C) Gas 5 for about 45 minutes – no stirring needed.

Serves: 4

DO-PIAZA
Meat and Onion Curry

A North Indian dish, Do (two) Piaza (onions) gets its name because onions appear twice in the cooking process. The first batch is fried and the second goes in raw later. Some recipes claim that the onion quantity should be twice that of the meat, and if you love onion you can do this, but this recipe achieves a sweetish savoury taste with less. You could use pork, beef, mutton, lamb or chicken etc.

3 lb (1.4 kg) chicken cut in pieces, or 1½ lb (675 g) lean meat, cubed

1 lb (450 g) onions, finely chopped

4 cloves garlic, finely chopped

½ cup ghee or oil

5 fl oz (150 ml) yoghurt

1 lb (450 g) onions, thinly sliced

4 fresh tomatoes, halved

1 tablespoon chopped fresh coriander or parsley

salt

Spices
6 cloves
1 brown cardamom
2 inch (5 cm) cinnamon
½ teaspoon ground ginger
1 teaspoon turmeric
1 teaspoon chilli powder
1 teaspoon garam masala

SP Spice pack available

1 Remove the skin from the chicken pieces, and cut any fat off the meat.
2 Fry the finely chopped onion (the first quantity) and garlic until golden in the ghee or oil.
3 Fold in the *spices* and stir-fry about 5 minutes.
4 Combine mixture with meat or poultry, the yoghurt and a cup of water, and put it all in a casserole dish. Place in preheated oven at 350°F (180°C) Gas 4, and cook for 20 minutes.
5 Add and mix in the raw thinly sliced onion (the second quantity), and tomatoes and coriander or parsley. Salt to taste. Raise heat to 425°F (220°C) Gas 7, and cook for a further 40 minutes or so.

Serves: 4

JAL FARAJEE or FREYZI
Cold Meat Curry

The idea that curry is for left-overs is quite wrong. But here is one way to use up the remnants of the Sunday joint. Serve with chupattis and pickles.

1 portion Curry Gravy (see pages 34–35)
1 small onion, finely chopped
1 clove garlic, finely chopped
mustard or vegetable oil
1–1½ lb (450–675 g) cooked beef, lamb or chicken etc

up to 8 oz (225 g) cooked vegetables (roast or boiled potatoes, peas, carrots etc)
salt

1 Make one of the simple curry gravies from Chapter 2, or use a good bottled curry paste.
2 Fry the onion and garlic in the oil until golden.
3 Add all the other ingredients to the pan. Mix well and heat thoroughly, over a gentle to medium heat.

Serves: 4

KORMA

True kormas are spicy, not hot, and a Moghul creation. Their special feature is a creamy sauce with nuts and saffron. They can be made with chicken, duck, lamb, beef or mutton, and should be served with plain or pullao rice (see pages 122–123).

1½ lb (675 g) poultry or meat

½ cup cashew nuts or almonds (or mixture)

½ inch (1.25 cm) fresh ginger, chopped

1 clove garlic, chopped

2 green chillies (optional)

½ teaspoon saffron

2 tablespoons milk, warmed

1 tablespoon ghee

2 tablespoons sunflower or corn oil

1 medium onion, chopped

3 fl oz (75 ml) yoghurt

3 fl oz (75 ml) double cream

½ cup chopped fresh coriander or parsley

salt

lemon juice (optional)

Spices

2 whole green cardamoms

3 whole cloves

1 inch (2.5 cm) cassia bark

1 teaspoon coriander seeds

1 teaspoon white cummin seeds

SP *Spice pack available*

1 Cut the meat into 1 inch (2.5 cm) cubes (the poultry on or off the bone, to taste).

2 Blend the nuts, ginger, garlic and chillies into a coarse paste with ¼ pint (150 ml) water.

3 Soak the saffron in warm milk for 10 minutes.

4 Heat the ghee and oil together, then fry the *spices* then the onion until golden. Add the nut paste and yoghurt, and cook for 10 minutes or so.

5 Add the meat, mixing it in well. Simmer for about 1 hour or until the meat is tender. Add water bit by bit if needed.

6 About 10 minutes before serving, squeeze the saffron strands in their bowl to get the most colour out of them then add in, with the milk. Add the double cream, fresh coriander or parsley and salt to taste. Serve with lemon juice if liked.

Serves: 4

Mild

MEDIUM CURRY, RESTAURANT STYLE

If there is a 'standard' curry at the Indian restaurant, then this recipe must be it. I hope it enables you to capture that 'restaurant flavour'. Remember to get a good creamy texture in the early stages of cooking by using the onion purée method (see page 30). Good luck, and when you've mastered it, who knows, maybe your local takeaway will become redundant!

1½ lb (675 g) lean lamb or chicken
½ cup vegetable oil
1 cup onion purée (see page 30)
1 tablespoon tomato purée

Spices 1
1 teaspoon cummin, ground
1 teaspoon coriander, ground
1 teaspoon turmeric
1 teaspoon paprika
1 teaspoon chilli powder (more if you like heat)
1 teaspoon ground ginger
1 teaspoon garlic powder

Spices 2
1 teaspoon garam masala
1 dessertspoon dry fenugreek leaves

SP *Spice pack available*

1 Cut any fat off the lamb, and skin the chicken, on or off the bone. Cut both into cubes of about 2 inches (5 cm).

2 Heat the oil and fry the onion purée until it is good and hot (don't let it stick).

3 While this is happening, add a little water to *spices 1* to make a paste, and preheat the oven to 375°F (190°C) Gas 5.

4 Add the paste to the hot onion purée, and stir continuously. Reduce the heat if it starts to stick. Take about 5–8 minutes over this (the bhoona operation), as it is important that the spices are cooked and the water content removed. When the oil floats to the top it is done.

5 Put the meat and onion and tomato purées into a casserole dish, stir, and put in the oven. Cook for 45 minutes.

6 Stir and add *spices 2*. Cook on a further 10 minutes then serve.

Serves: 4

MADRAS

Chicken, Turkey, Beef or Mutton Curry

Although this curry features prominently on most Indian restaurant menus, you won't find it in many cookbooks. This is a typical curry from South India where they don't come much hotter.

1½ lb (675 g) meat or poultry
½ cup corn or vegetable oil
1 large onion, sliced long and thin
14 oz (400 g) tin tomatoes
2 tablespoons tomato purée
2 tablespoons fresh lemon or (better) lime juice
salt
knob of ghee

Spices 1
4 dry red chillies (more if you like heat)
½ teaspoon black pepper, ground (more if you like heat)
½ teaspoon chilli powder (more if you like heat)
1 teaspoon white cummin seeds
1 teaspoon fenugreek seeds
1 teaspoon turmeric
2 white cardamoms

Spices 2
1 dessertspoon garam masala
1 dessertspoon dry fenugreek leaves

SP **Spice pack available**

1 Remove fat or skin from meat, and cut in 1 inch (2.5 cm) cubes. Leave poultry on the bone if liked. Fry in the oil to seal, then remove with a slotted spoon and leave to one side.

2 Fry the onion in the same oil until golden then add *spices 1*, cooking a further 5 minutes. Add the tinned tomatoes and purée and mix well. Cook for 10 minutes or so. *

3 Put into a casserole in a preheated oven, at 400°F (200°C) Gas 6, and cook for 45–60 minutes. Stir half-way through cooking time.

4 Add the lemon or lime juice and *spices 2* and simmer for 10 minutes. Add a little water at any stage if it dries up. Salt to taste, then add a knob of ghee just before serving (this just makes it taste better!). It will keep well overnight, or can be frozen.

Serves: 4

VINDALOO

Beef, Pork, Chicken or Duck Curry

This dish, from Goa and South India, is really hot and sour. Pork was the traditional meat to use, but any vindaloo tastes delicious. Vindaloo, to most restaurateurs, means simply a very hot curry. They have also created Bindaloo (hotter) and Tindaloo (even hotter). This recipe was given to me in Goa and it is the real thing. The Goans reckon that the longer you leave it to marinate after cooking the better it tastes.

1½ lb (675 g) meat or poultry

½ cup vinegar

8 oz (225 g) potatoes, peeled and cut in 1 inch (2.5 cm) cubes

4 tablespoons mustard or corn oil

1 large onion, finely chopped

4 cloves garlic, finely chopped (more if you like)

2 inch (5 cm) fresh ginger, finely chopped

2 medium tomatoes, quartered

1 tablespoon desiccated coconut

Spices 1 (Vindaloo Masala)

3 cloves, ground

1 brown cardamom, ground

1 inch (2.5 cm) cassia bark, ground

1 teaspoon white cummin seeds

1 teaspoon fenugreek seeds

½ teaspoon asafoetida

Spices 2

6 red chillies (more if you can cope!)

3 green cardamoms

1 teaspoon black mustard seeds

½ teaspoon black cummin seeds

2 or 3 bay leaves

Spices 3

1½ teaspoons turmeric

1 teaspoon chilli powder

1 teaspoon cummin, ground

SP *Spice pack available*

1   Cut any fat off the meat, skin poultry, and cut into 1 inch (2.5 cm) cubes. Mix *spices 1* in the vinegar, and leave for 10 minutes. Mix these spices with the meat and potato, and leave to marinate overnight or for a minimum of 3 hours.

2   Heat the oil to medium and put in *spices 2*. Cook 5 minutes then add the onion, garlic and ginger. Cook for a further 10–15 minutes, stirring to prevent sticking (add a little water if necessary).

3   Add the tomatoes, meat/potato/marinade mixture, and *spices 3*. Cook for a minimum of 10 minutes.

4 Put the lot into a casserole dish and in a preheated oven at 400°F (200°C) Gas 6. Cook for 45 minutes, or longer if you wish. Stir occasionally. Either serve it when you're ready, or let it cool and stand overnight to increase its pungency. Garnish with desiccated coconut.

Serves: 4

PHALL

The Hottest Curry of All

This curry is an incendiary hot recipe for the fire eaters only – it must not be eaten by the unsuspecting. It is a very hot curry indeed, producing an attractive red sauce. Serve with plain rice, and, if you dare, chilli pickle and fresh chilli chutney (pages 142).

1½ lb (675 g) meat or poultry
1 large onion, finely chopped
8 cloves garlic, finely chopped
1 oz (25 g) fresh ginger, finely
   chopped
3 tablespoons ghee or oil
14 oz (400 g) tin tomatoes
1 tablespoon tomato ketchup
1 tablespoon tomato purée
12 fresh or dried chillies (or
   more)
salt

Spices
1 teaspoon cummin, ground
1 teaspoon coriander, ground
3 teaspoons chilli powder
1 teaspoon dry fenugreek
   leaves
1 teaspoon garam masala

SP *Spice pack available*

I Chop the meat and fry onion, garlic and ginger until golden in half the ghee or oil.

2 Mix the *spices* with a little water to make a paste. Add to the onion mixture, and cook for 10 minutes.

3 Add the tomato (tinned, ketchup and purée) and chillies. Cook for a further 10 minutes.

4 Meanwhile fry the meat in a separate pan in remaining ghee or oil, until sealed (5–10 minutes).

5 Combine all ingredients in a casserole dish and cook in preheated oven at 400°F (200°C) Gas 6 for 45–60 minutes. This curry can be left to marinate overnight or it can be frozen.

Serves: 4

6
FISH & SEAFOOD CURRIES

India has a coastline stretching for many thousands of miles. Exotic seafood is prolific and cheap – lobsters, crabs, vast giant prawns, shrimps and all sorts of fish, ordinary and weird (in fact anything that swims or lives in water) are cooked and curried. Much of it may not be to our taste – and even if it might be it is not possible to obtain the fresh ingredients. Add to that the fact that 90 per cent of the 'Indian' restaurateurs over here are from Pakistan or Bangladesh where the fish tradition is not as developed as that of meat and vegetables, and the result is very little choice on the menu. Here is a small but varied choice of fish and seafood dishes, which once you try them, I'm sure you'll choose regularly.

FISH MOLLEE or MOULI

You're unlikely to find this dish at your local Indian restaurant. It comes from Sri Lanka where they add chillies at fire extinguisher level to the very delicate flavouring. Here chillies are optional.

3 tablespoons warm milk
2 teaspoons wine vinegar
1 large onion, chopped
1 clove garlic, finely chopped (optional)
2 tablespoons mustard or sunflower oil
coconut milk (if available)
1½ lb (675 g) white fish, skinned and boned
2 green chillies, chopped (optional)
salt
lemon juice

Spices
1 tablespoon desiccated coconut
½ teaspoon turmeric
¼ teaspoon ground ginger
¼ teaspoon asafoetida
2 black peppercorns
¼ teaspoon saffron strands

SP *Spice pack available*

I Soak the *spices* in the warm milk and the vinegar for 30 minutes or so.

2 Fry the onion and garlic (if used) in the oil until golden.

3 Add the pre-soaked spices and half a cup of coconut milk (or water). When hot, add the fish with the chillies (if used) and keep the sauce fairly fluid while cooking by adding water as required.

4 Cook until the fish is tender – 10–15 minutes or so – and add salt to taste. As soon as cooked, sprinkle with lemon juice, and serve with plain rice and accompaniments.

Serves: 4

FRIED MACKEREL

This recipe is another favourite home-cooking dish which never seems to turn up on the restaurant menu. Why not, I cannot say. I'm sure it will be a regular with you.

4 medium mackerel	**Spices**
juice of 2 lemons	1 teaspoon turmeric
½ cup vegetable oil	1 teaspoon chilli powder
1 cup chopped fresh coriander	1 teaspoon garlic powder
salt	½ teaspoon black cummin seeds
	½ teaspoon asafoetida

1 Top, tail, scale and fillet the fish.
2 Make a paste of the *spices* with the lemon juice. Marinate fish in the paste for an hour.
3 Heat the oil in a frying pan, and fry the fish along with all the spice paste. It will be ready in about 5–10 minutes.
4 Sprinkle with fresh coriander, salt to taste and serve with lemon wedges and chupattis (page 132).

Serves: 4

GOAN CRAB

Crabs are prolific in Goa, that exotic place south of Bombay where blue seas lap white sands and reflect green palm trees – ah me! Capture a bit of this with a delightful 'fish course', or cold starter, which is ridiculously simple to make. Buy cooked crab from the fishmonger.

4 oz (115 g) fresh shredded white crab meat	**Spices**
	½ teaspoon turmeric
2 oz (50 g) fresh brown crab meat	½ teaspoon cummin, ground
	½ teaspoon paprika
1 teaspoon lemon juice	⅛ teaspoon asafoetida
fresh coriander or parsley	½ teaspoon garam masala

1 Make the *spices* into a paste using a little water and the lemon juice, then mix the crab meats and the paste.
2 Serve cold in small dishes, garnished with parsley or fresh coriander.

Serves: 4

PRAWN CURRY
(or Lobster, Crab, Scallops, Scampi)

This seafood curry comes traditionally from the south of India, Sri Lanka and Malaya. People there usually like their food searingly hot. This recipe spares you that, and it is very delicate. But you can add chillies to taste to capture the atmosphere! It comes out a bright lemon yellow colour with contrasting green pepper stripes. Serve with plain rice and chutneys.

1½ lb (675 g) seafood of choice

2 tablespoons ghee or sunflower oil

1 large onion, finely chopped

1 clove garlic, finely chopped

2 or more fresh green chillies, chopped (optional)

½ teaspoon saffron strands

2 tablespoons warm milk

1 small green pepper, cut into strips

1 teaspoon granulated sugar

salt

1 tablespoon chopped fresh coriander or parsley

Spices

1 teaspoon turmeric

1 teaspoon coriander, ground

½ teaspoon black pepper, ground

1 tablespoon desiccated coconut

[SP] *Spice pack available*

1 Prepare the seafood: shell, clean, chop if necessary.

2 Heat the ghee and fry the onion and garlic until golden.

3 Add *spices* and simmer for 2 minutes. Add the optional chillies.

4 Put the saffron strands into the warm milk, let stand for 10 minutes, then mash to get the most colour out.

5 Add the seafood to the pan with the onion and spices etc, and simmer for about 15 minutes.

6 Blanch the green pepper strips for about 1 minute to remove the acidity, then add to the pan along with the saffron, milk, sugar and a little salt.

7 Cook a further 5–15 minutes until you are ready to serve. About 3 minutes before serving sprinkle the coriander or parsley on top. The dish should be neither too thick nor too runny (add water if too thick and rice flour if too runny).

Serves: 4

PATIA ✓

Sweet and Sour Seafood Curry

Recipes for this dish do not appear in most Indian cookery books, but it is a well known favourite on many an Indian restaurant menu. The curry should be sweet and sour in a thick, dark brown dryish gravy. Prawns are ideal but you can use shrimps, lobster, scallops, crab, crayfish etc or any mixture.

1½ lb (675 g) seafood
3 tablespoons yoghurt
1 medium onion, roughly
    chopped
2 cloves garlic
1 inch (2.5 cm) fresh ginger
2 tablespoons mustard oil
2 tablespoons tamarind juice
    (see page 16) *lemon juice OK*
1 tablespoon brown sugar
1 tablespoon honey
1 tablespoon vinegar
1 tablespoon tomato ketchup
salt

Spices 1
½ teaspoon mustard seeds
½ teaspoon fennel seeds *(careful)*
½ teaspoon cummin seeds
½ teaspoon fenugreek seeds

Spices 2
½ teaspoon turmeric
1 teaspoon coriander, ground
½ teaspoon cummin, ground
2 teaspoons paprika

SP **Spice pack available**

1 Prepare the seafood, and heat briefly, strain and keep to one side.
2 Pound or blend yoghurt, onion, garlic and ginger plus 4 tablespoons water to a paste.
3 Heat mustard oil and fry *spices 1* for 1–2 minutes. Add yoghurt and onion blend, and fry until golden (15 minutes).
4 Add *spices 2* and cook for a further 3–5 minutes.
5 Meanwhile, to the tamarind juice add the sugar, honey, vinegar and tomato ketchup.
6 Add all this to the fried mixture, and cook for 5–10 minutes. Add the seafood and salt and simmer until you have a thick, dark gravy (about 10 minutes).

Serves: 4

HOT PRAWN AND VEGETABLE CURRY

This dish is lightly but deliciously spiced, and makes a change from the usual type of curry.

4 oz (115 g) onion, finely chopped

2 small garlic cloves, finely chopped

1 tablespoon mustard or vegetable oil

½ cup tinned sweetcorn niblets (retain liquid from tin)

2 oz (50 g) creamed coconut, grated

1 lb (450 g) prawns

juice of ½ lemon

1 teaspoon sugar

½ teaspoon salt

1 cup cooked, chopped broccoli

1 tablespoon finely chopped fresh coriander or parsley

Spices

1 teaspoon cloves, freshly ground

1 teaspoon cinnamon, freshly ground

1 level teaspoon turmeric

2 teaspoons chilli powder

1 Fry the onion and garlic in oil until golden.

2 Add the ground cloves and cinnamon and cook for a minute until well mixed.

3 Make the sweetcorn liquid up to 1 cup with water. Add to onions, with turmeric, chilli powder and coconut. Cook gently for 5 minutes.

4 Add prawns, lemon juice, sugar and salt, sweetcorn and broccoli. Cook for 7–10 minutes, simmering very gently.

5 Sprinkle with coriander or parsley before serving. Add water if necessary during cooking (if you use frozen prawns you may need less stock because frozen prawns contain more water than fresh).

***Serves:** 4*

7

NON-MEAT CURRIES

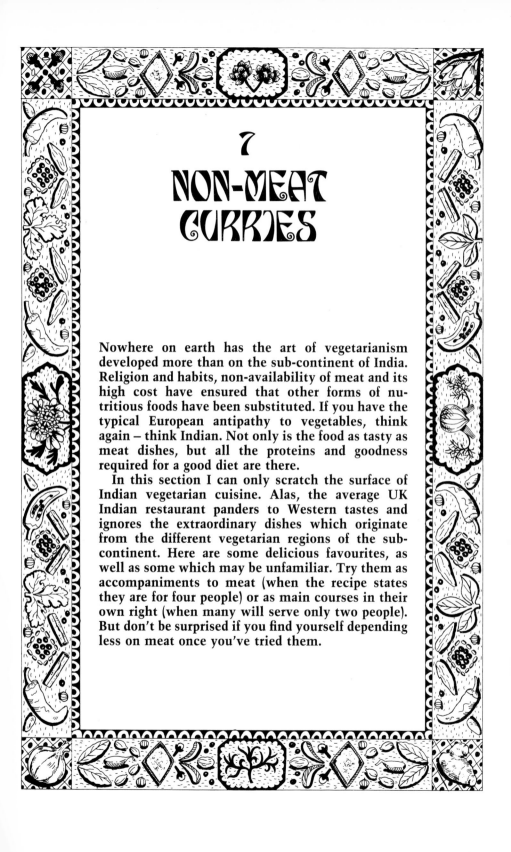

Nowhere on earth has the art of vegetarianism developed more than on the sub-continent of India. Religion and habits, non-availability of meat and its high cost have ensured that other forms of nutritious foods have been substituted. If you have the typical European antipathy to vegetables, think again – think Indian. Not only is the food as tasty as meat dishes, but all the proteins and goodness required for a good diet are there.

In this section I can only scratch the surface of Indian vegetarian cuisine. Alas, the average UK Indian restaurant panders to Western tastes and ignores the extraordinary dishes which originate from the different vegetarian regions of the sub-continent. Here are some delicious favourites, as well as some which may be unfamiliar. Try them as accompaniments to meat (when the recipe states they are for four people) or as main courses in their own right (when many will serve only two people). But don't be surprised if you find yourself depending less on meat once you've tried them.

BAIGAN BURTA

Roast Aubergine Curry

A sweetish, attractively coloured curry, and it is well worth the trouble it takes to prepare.

4 whole aubergines
4 fl oz (115 ml) yoghurt
8 oz (225 g) onions, sliced
   lengthwise
3 cloves garlic, finely chopped
1 oz (25 g) fresh ginger, finely
   chopped
¾ cup vegetable oil
12 oz (350 g) fresh small
   tomatoes, halved
8 oz (225 g) small peas
salt

Garnish
2 dessertspoons chopped fresh
   coriander or parsley
cashew or pistachio nuts and
   small button mushrooms

Spices 1
3 green cardamoms
1 inch (2.5 cm) cassia bark
3 cloves
1 teaspoon paprika
½ teaspoon turmeric
½ teaspoon chilli powder
½ teaspoon coriander, ground
½ teaspoon black pepper,
   ground

Spices 2
1 dessertspoon garam masala

1 Make a small slit in each aubergine, then grill lightly for 30 minutes (on foil in the grill pan). Don't let them burn. They should look wrinkled and darker.

2 Soak them in cold water and scoop out the flesh, discarding the skin. Mash the flesh with the yoghurt. (This can be done in advance and chilled.)

3 Fry the onions, garlic and ginger in ½ cup oil until golden, then add half the tomatoes and continue frying.

4 Add *spices 1* and peas and fry for 10 minutes. Stir frequently.

5 Add the aubergine/yoghurt mixture, and salt to taste.

6 In a separate pan heat remaining oil and fry the aubergine mixture. Cook for 5 minutes before adding *spices 2*. Cook for a further 5 minutes, stirring frequently.

7 Place the curry in a flattish dish, and arrange the remaining tomato halves on top. Sprinkle with the garnish ingredients, and serve.

Serves: *4 as an accompaniment*

BHAJEE
Mixed Vegetable Curry

This is a standard restaurant recipe which makes an ideal accompaniment to any meat and rice main course. You can vary the vegetables.

10 oz (300 g) potatoes
4 oz (115 g) carrots
4 oz (115 g) turnips (if available)
3 tablespoons vegetable oil
1 large onion, finely chopped
4 oz (115 g) tomatoes, tinned or fresh
4 oz (115 g) peas
salt

Spices
1 teaspoon turmeric
1 teaspoon cummin, ground
1 teaspoon coriander, ground
1 teaspoon chilli powder
2 teaspoons garlic powder
2 teaspoons paprika

SP **Spice pack available**

1 Wash, peel and chop the potatoes, carrots and turnips, then blanch in boiling water for about 5 minutes.

2 Mix the *spices* with a little water to form a stiffish paste.

3 Heat the oil, fry the onion until golden, then add the paste. Fry for 5 minutes or so.

4 Combine blanched vegetables with the fried onion and spices, then add the tomatoes and peas. Simmer until cooked – about 15–20 minutes – adding salt to taste.

Serves: *4*

UNDUI

Vegetable Curry

A delicate but exotic mixture of selected vegetables. Fenugreek and fennel seeds are said to be aphrodisiac – try them and see!

4 oz (115 g) *each* of the following vegetables: carrots, turnips, white pumpkin, green peas, white radish, broad beans, spinach

1 large onion

1 cup vegetable oil

1 inch (2.5 cm) fresh ginger, pounded to paste

2 cloves garlic, pounded to paste

4 fl oz (115 ml) yoghurt

1 green chilli, chopped

salt and pepper to taste

Spices

1 inch (2.5 cm) cinnamon

5 cardamom seeds

5 cloves

2 bay leaves

1 teaspoon cummin seeds

1 teaspoon fennel seeds

1 teaspoon fenugreek seeds

1 teaspoon turmeric

1 teaspoon chilli powder

1 teaspoon coriander, ground

1 teaspoon garam masala

1 Chop all relevant vegetables into ½ inch (1.5 cm) cubes, pod the peas and beans, and roughly chop the spinach. Chop the onion finely.

2 Blanch all vegetables except onions and spinach for a few minutes in boiling water.

3 Heat oil, add onion, and cook until golden brown.

4 Mix ginger and garlic pastes with the yoghurt and add to the browned onions. Cook for 5 minutes on moderate heat, then add the *spices*. Continue cooking until the fat rises to the surface.

5 Add all the vegetables, including the chilli, but excluding the spinach. Add the spinach when all the other vegetables are cooked (about 10–15 minutes), and simmer for a further 5 minutes or so.

Serves: 4

DOSA or DOSAI
Savoury Pancake

Pancakes made from ground rice and dhal, filled with potato. Serve with Sambar (page 101) and Coconut Chutney (page 145). In South India this is a breakfast or lunch dish, but I consider it good at any time!

4 tablespoons rice flour
1½ tablespoons urid dhal flour
about 6 tablespoons milk

Filling
1 teaspoon toor dhal (soaked overnight)
mustard or sunflower oil
1 large onion, thinly sliced
4 medium potatoes, diced
2 green chillies, chopped (optional)
salt
2 tablespoons chopped fresh coriander or parsley

Spices 1
1 teaspoon mustard seeds

Spices 2
1 teaspoon turmeric
1 teaspoon paprika
1 teaspoon garam masala
1 teaspoon dry fenugreek leaves

SP *Spice pack available*

1 To begin the pancakes, blend the rice and dhal flours into a stiff paste with as little water as possible. Stand overnight in a warm place to ferment. Soak the dhal for the filling at the same time.

2 The next day, to make the filling, heat 3 tablespoons of the oil in a saucepan, add *spices 1* and when the seeds start popping, add sliced onion and cook until golden.

3 Add potato, chillies, dhal, *spices 2*, salt and a little water. Cook on medium heat until potatoes are done. Keep mixture quite dry, but don't let it burn. When cooked add fresh coriander. Put to one side.

4 Now make the pancakes. Add enough milk to the pancake paste to make a normal pancake consistency – quite runny – but don't make it *too* thin. Salt to taste.

5 Heat 1 teaspoon of oil in a non-stick frying pan, and ladle in a little batter. Cook on both sides. The pancakes should be about 6–8 inches (15–20 cm) in diameter.

6 Remove from frying pan, and spoon some of the potato mixture onto each pancake. Roll it up, round the mixture, and store in warm oven. Use up remaining batter in same way, storing pancakes in oven until ready to serve. Any left-over potato filling can be served separately at the table if you wish.

***Makes:* 8**

Sema masala
Beans Curry

Beans curry? And why not? Beans of various types and sizes do grow in India. This recipe uses beans which you can get over here, and the combination in this recipe is especially interesting (but you can use any type of fresh or frozen bean).

**8 oz (225 g) runner beans,
  fresh or frozen**
**8 oz (225 g) podded broad
  beans, fresh or frozen**
2 tablespoons sunflower oil
**1 medium onion, finely
  chopped**
**1 cup chopped fresh coriander
  or parsley**
salt

Spices 1
½ teaspoon wild onion seeds
½ teaspoon sesame seeds
½ teaspoon fennel seeds
½ teaspoon cummin seeds

Spices 2
½ teaspoon coriander, ground
½ teaspoon chilli powder

1 Wash and string the runners, and chop to shape of your choice.

2 Heat the oil, and add *spices 1*. Fry until they change colour (about 2–3 minutes), then add the onion. Fry until translucent (5–10 minutes).

3 Add *spices 2* and cook for a further 5 minutes.

4 Meanwhile blanch both the beans in a little boiling water for about 3 minutes. Strain and keep the water.

5 Add the beans to the fried items and simmer until cooked – 15–20 minutes maximum. Add some 'bean water' if it looks a little dry.

6 Add the coriander or parsley and salt to taste about 3 minutes before cooking is completed.

Serves: 4

SAMBAR

This is a mixture of vegetables in a fairly runny sauce (the consistency is like minestrone soup), which is served as an accompaniment to Dosas. It can also be added to mixed vegetable curries or dhal dishes.

This quantity will probably be too much for one meal, so you can freeze the remainder for another meal. (The tinned vegetables give a particularly nice flavour because the brine contributes so well to the flavour of the stock.)

1 tablespoon masoor dhal (red lentils)

1 medium onion, in long thin slices

8 oz (225 g) peas

14 oz (400 g) tin mixed, diced vegetables

2 tablespoons ghee

1 teaspoon lemon juice (or more to taste)

1 tablespoon desiccated coconut

salt

Spices (Sambar Masala)

1 tablespoon channa dhal, ground

1 tablespoon urid dhal, ground

1 tablespoon toor dhal, ground

1 tablespoon turmeric

2 tablespoons coriander seeds

1 tablespoon cummin seeds

½ teaspoon black pepper, ground

½ teaspoon chilli powder

SP *Spice pack available*

1 Boil the lentils until fairly soft (about 20 minutes). Add the onion, peas and tinned vegetables towards the end of cooking time. Use about 1 pint (600 ml) of water for this and leave slightly *under*-cooked. Strain and keep the stock.

2 While vegetables are cooking, soak the *spices* in a cup with enough water to make a thin paste.

3 Heat the ghee, add the spice paste and fry for 2 minutes or so.

4 Add the lemon juice, coconut and vegetables. Add the vegetable stock bit by bit, and simmer for 5 minutes, or until the vegetables, especially the lentils, are thoroughly cooked. Salt and serve.

Serves: 6–8

CABBAGE FOOGATH

White, red or green cabbage fried in onions as a simple accompanying dish. You can use other vegetables if you prefer.

1 medium onion, sliced
1 clove garlic, chopped
vegetable oil
1 cabbage, shredded

4 green chillies, chopped
1 cup fresh grated coconut or
  1 tablespoon desiccated
salt

1 Fry the onion and garlic in oil until golden.

2 Add the cabbage, chillies and coconut and stir-fry (use a wok or karahi) until tender.

3 Salt to taste, and serve as soon as possible.

Serves: 4–6

GOBHI KASHMIRI
Kashmir Cauliflower

Cauliflower cooked in a rich sauce of nuts and spices. This is a dish from Kashmir, where dishes are usually red in colour because of the extensive use of ratan jot, a red herbal food colouring. The richness of many Kashmiri dishes is due to the use of nuts, grown in the north.

1 cup vegetable oil or ghee
4 oz (115 g) onions, sliced
2 cloves garlic, pounded into
  paste
1 inch (2.5 cm) fresh ginger,
  pounded into paste
4 oz (115 g) tomatoes, chopped
1 lb (450 g) cauliflower florets
2 tablespoons cashew nuts
1 tablespoon pistachio nuts
1 tablespoon sultanas
salt
1 tablespoon chopped fresh
  coriander

Spices
1 teaspoon cummin seeds
3 teaspoons turmeric
½ teaspoon chilli powder
1 teaspoon garam masala
1 teaspoon ratan jot (alkenet
  root) or ¼ teaspoon red food
  colouring

1 Heat the oil in a large flameproof casserole and add the onions, garlic, ginger and *spices*. Cook for 7–8 minutes.

2 Add tomatoes, and cook for 5 minutes.

3 Add cauliflower florets and ¾ pint (450 ml) water. Cook with lid on for 10 minutes or so.

4 Add cashews, pistachios and sultanas, season to taste, heat through, then remove from heat. Garnish with chopped coriander just before serving.

Serves: 4

CAULIFLOWER CURRY

This can be served as a vegetarian main dish (with rice and dhal) or as an accompaniment to meat dishes.

1 cauliflower
8 oz (225 g) peas, fresh or frozen
4 medium potatoes, peeled and quartered
1 medium onion, cut into long thin strips
1 clove garlic, finely chopped
1 inch (2.5 cm) fresh ginger, finely chopped
sunflower oil
14 oz (400 g) tin tomatoes
salt

Spices
3 whole cloves
1 teaspoon coriander seeds
1 teaspoon cummin seeds
½ teaspoon black mustard seeds
1 teaspoon garam masala
1 dessertspoon dry fenugreek leaves

SP *Spice pack available*

1 Separate the cauliflower into florets and set aside. Pod fresh peas.

2 Par-boil or steam the potatoes until half-cooked (about 8 minutes).

3 Fry the onion, garlic and ginger in oil until golden, then add *spices*.

4 Put in the potatoes, cauliflower florets, peas and tomatoes, cover and cook for 15–20 minutes. Add a little water as it starts to dry up but *do not over-cook*, as you want the vegetables to still have a little crispness or 'bite'.

Serves: 4

CAULIFLOWER KORMA CURRY

The spicy creaminess of the Korma sauce goes deliciously with cauliflower.

1½ lb (675 g) cauliflower
½ cup cashew nuts or almonds (or mixture)
½ inch (1.25 cm) fresh ginger, chopped
1 clove garlic, chopped
2 green chillies (optional)
½ teaspoon saffron strands
2 tablespoons warm milk
1 tablespoon ghee
2 tablespoons sunflower or corn oil
1 medium onion, chopped
3 fl oz (75 ml) yoghurt
3 fl oz (75 ml) double cream
½ cup chopped fresh coriander or parsley
salt

Spices
2 whole green cardamoms
3 whole cloves
1 inch (2.5 cm) cassia bark
1 teaspoon coriander seeds
1 teaspoon white cummin seeds

SP **Spice pack available**

1   Cut the cauliflower into florets, and set to one side.

2   Blend the nuts, ginger, garlic, *spices*, chillies and ¼ pint (150 ml) water into a coarse paste.

3   Soak the saffron in the warm milk for 10 minutes.

4   Heat the ghee and oil together, and fry the onion until golden. Add the spice paste and yoghurt, and cook for 10 minutes or so.

5   Add the cauliflower, mixing it in well. Cook for about 15 minutes (add water if necessary).

6   About 10 minutes before serving, squeeze the saffron strands in their bowl to get the most colour out of them, and mix into the pan with the milk. Add the double cream, fresh coriander or parsley, and salt to taste. Serve with some lemon juice if you like.

***Serves:** 4*

KOYA GOBHI MATTAR
White Curry

This dish is nice and spicy, yet the sauce is white. Try it as a very attractive accompaniment or as a vegetarian main meal.

1 medium onion, finely
  chopped
sesame or sunflower oil
½ cup cashew nuts, blanched
  to remove skins and ground
½ cup double cream
2 tablespoons milk powder
1 large cauliflower, in florets,
  par-boiled
1 cup peas, fresh or frozen
salt
1 tablespoon chopped fresh
  coriander

Spices
½ teaspoon fennel seeds,
  coarsely ground
1 teaspoon sesame seeds
½ teaspoon coriander, ground

1 Fry the onion in oil until translucent, about 10 minutes.

2 Meanwhile make a paste from the nuts, cream, milk powder and *spices*. Add water if needed to get a thick consistency.

3 Combine the onion, paste, cauliflower and peas. Simply heat through, simmering for a maximum of 10 minutes. Add a little salt, and some water if needed. Garnish with fresh coriander, and serve very fresh and hot.

Serves: 4

DoroO
Celery Curry

This is, I confess, an invention of mine. Celery is so easy to get in the UK (and elsewhere) and it cooks well – so why not a light curry?

1 lb (450 g) celery
2 tablespoons sunflower oil
2 cloves garlic, finely chopped
1 tablespoon fresh mint
  leaves or ½ teaspoon
  bottled mint
1 tablespoon chopped fresh
  coriander or parsley
2 fresh chillies, chopped

Spices
½ teaspoon fennel seeds
1 teaspoon sesame seeds
½ teaspoon poppy seeds
½ teaspoon mustard seeds

1 Wash and chop the celery into bite-sized chunks. Blanch in boiling water for 2 minutes (or steam), and retain the water after straining.

2 Heat the oil, and fry the *spices* for 2 minutes.

3 Add the garlic, celery, mint, coriander or parsley and chillies, plus a little celery water if needed.

4 Simmer for about 15 minutes, until the celery is cooked to your liking, then serve fresh and hot.

Serves: 4

Makhani Kumbi
Crusty Mushrooms

This dish provides a pleasant taste and texture contrast to curry dishes. The mushrooms are slow cooked and the result should be dry and crusty.

8 oz (225 g) button
  mushrooms
1½ tablespoons ghee
1 tablespoon chopped fresh
  chives
salt

Spices
2 white cardamoms
2 teaspoons paprika

SP *Spice pack available*

1 Wash and dry mushrooms if dirty, but don't peel.

2 Cut the cardamoms open, separate the seeds, and discard the husks.

3 Heat 1 tablespoon ghee in frying pan, medium to hot, and fry the cardamom seeds for 2 minutes.

4 Put in mushrooms, ensure they are well coated with ghee, then turn them rounded top down in the pan. Simmer for 15 minutes.

5 Add a little more ghee, turn the mushrooms, rounded top *up*, and sprinkle on the paprika. This will form a crust on the mushrooms as it cooks (a further 15–20 minutes on low heat).

6 Add chopped chives and salt just before serving.

Serves: 4

GAJAR, MATTAR KI KAJU
Carrot, Pea and Nut Curry

This is a Bengali recipe which I encountered at a restaurant in India. It uses panch phoran (see page 32), and should produce a delicate and lightly cooked dish.

1 lb (450 g) carrots
8 oz (225 g) peas, fresh or frozen
2 tablespoons sunflower oil
1 medium onion, sliced in 1 inch (2.5 cm) strips
1 clove garlic, finely chopped
½ cup cashew nuts
salt

Spices 1
1 teaspoon panch phoran (see page 32)

Spices 2
½ teaspoon turmeric
½ teaspoon coriander, ground
½ teaspoon black pepper, ground
1 teaspoon paprika

1 Wash, scrape and cut the carrots into small chunks, then blanch them in a little boiling water for 3 minutes (reserve the water). Pod fresh peas.

2 Heat the oil, and fry the panch phoran (*spices 1*) until the seeds pop, about 2 minutes.

3 Add the onion and garlic, and fry for 10 minutes.

4 Add *spices 2* and a little carrot water. Fry until the oil rises, stirring frequently, for about 5–10 minutes.

5 Add the carrots, peas and nuts and more carrot water if needed. Simmer for 20 minutes or so, adding a little salt, until the vegetables are cooked to taste.

Serves: 4

PANCH AMRIT
Nut Curry

An ambrosial recipe, which is a mixture of selected nuts prepared in a special peanut sauce.

1 cup vegetable oil or ghee
1 large onion, chopped
4 oz (115 g) desiccated coconut
3 oz (75 g) peanuts, finely chopped (1)
2 green chillies, chopped
1 inch (2.5 cm) fresh ginger, finely chopped
1 clove garlic, finely chopped
1 cup coconut water
salt
2 cups water
4 oz (115 g) dry sliced fresh coconut
4 oz (115 g) cashew nuts
4 oz (115 g) almonds
4 oz (115 g) sultanas
4 oz (115 g) peanuts, whole (2)
about 1 tablespoon sugar
1 tablespoon chopped fresh coriander

Spices 1
2 teaspoons mustard seeds

Spices 2
1 teaspoon turmeric
1 teaspoon coriander, ground
1 teaspoon cummin, ground

1 Heat the fat and add chopped onion and mustard seeds (*spices 1*). Cook for 5 minutes.

2 Add desiccated coconut, finely chopped peanuts (1), chopped green chillies, ginger and garlic, coconut water, salt, 2 cups water and *spices 2*. Cook for 10–12 minutes.

3 Add the sliced dry coconut, cashew nuts, almonds, sultanas and peanuts (2). Cook for a further 10 minutes until the fat rises to the surface.

4 Add sugar before removing from the heat, and garnish with chopped coriander before serving.

Serves: *4*

BINDI BHAJEE
Okra Curry

*The okra is a vegetable native to India. Also known as bindi, or ladies'
fingers, it vaguely resembles a chilli in shape but is not hot. In fact it is
a type of bean, pale green, about 3–4 inches (7–10 cm) long. They are
not to everyone's taste, being a bit pithy, but if you can get hold of
them fresh, they do add the right ambiance to a meal! Avoid hard
scaly ones – they should be soft and pliable. (Tinned okra can be
obtained from The Curry Club Mail Order service.)*

12 oz (350 g) okra
3 tablespoons mustard oil
1 medium onion, finely
   chopped
2 cloves garlic, finely chopped
2 inch (5 cm) fresh ginger,
   finely chopped
4 oz (115 g) fresh or tinned
   tomatoes
1 green pepper, finely chopped
4 green chillies, finely
   chopped

Spices 1
1 teaspoon mustard seeds,
   slightly crushed
1 teaspoon coriander seeds,
   slightly crushed
½ teaspoon fenugreek seeds,
   slightly crushed

Spices 2
1 teaspoon turmeric
2 teaspoons cummin seeds
2 teaspoons paprika
½ teaspoon asafoetida

1 Wash the okra and cut off the stalks. Prick them two or three times
but don't chop them. Blanch in a little boiling water for at least 5
minutes. Strain and discard the water, which will be fairly sticky.
Wash the okra in cold water.

2 Heat the oil and fry *spices 1* for 2 or 3 minutes.

3 Add the onion, garlic and ginger and fry for 10 minutes. Stir
regularly.

4 Meanwhile make *spices 2* into a paste with a little water. Add to the
onion mix, and fry for a further 10 minutes.

5 Add the okra, tomatoes, green pepper, chillies and a little water, and
simmer for 30 minutes, adding water as needed. Salt and serve.

Serves: 4

BHARE TAMARTA PALAK
Tomatoes Stuffed with Spinach

Tomatoes in India grow large, firm and plum shaped – rather like the tinned Italian ones. Buy good fresh firm large Continental tomatoes.
   Restaurants tend not to serve this dish, because it is quite fiddly to make, but it is easy to prepare at home.

4 large tomatoes
2 tablespoons sunflower oil
1 small onion, chopped
2 cloves garlic, chopped
12 oz (350 g) spinach, fresh or frozen
4 oz (115 g) mashed potato
2 chillies, chopped

Spices
1 teaspoon turmeric
1 teaspoon garam masala
2 teaspoons paprika

1 Wash the tomatoes. Carefully cut off the top and scoop out the seeds and pulp, which you reserve.

2 Make a paste of the *spices* with a little water, and heat the oil.

3 Fry the onion and garlic for 10 minutes, then add the spice paste. Fry for a further 10 minutes, stirring frequently.

4 Very finely chop the spinach. Mix it with the mashed potato, chopped chillies, and the tomato pulp. Add to the onion and spices and fry for further 5 minutes. Allow to cool, then strain off excess liquid or oil if necessary.

5 When cool, stuff filling into the tomatoes, right to the top, and replace the 'lid'. (Freeze any spare filling.)

6 Preheat oven to 375°F (190°C) Gas 5 and place tomatoes on or in oven dish. Cover with lid or foil and cook for about 15–20 minutes (check to see if you are happy with softness of tomato). Serve on plain rice as an accompaniment, or main dish.

Serves: *4 as an accompaniment*
2 as a main dish

SAAG BHAJEE
Spinach Curry

*One green vegetable dish makes an interesting visual contrast.
Spinach curries well, but try cauliflower or white cabbage as well.*

1 lb (450 g) fresh or frozen
  spinach

1 dessertspoon sunflower oil

1 small onion, in long thin
  slices

1 small clove garlic, finely
  chopped

salt

knob of ghee

Spices

½ teaspoon cummin seeds

⅓ teaspoon garam masala

SP *Spice pack available*

I Wash fresh spinach several times to remove dirt, chop into strips,
and discard tough stalks. Boil (or steam) until tender in just the
water adhering to the leaves.

2 Heat oil in frying pan, medium to hot, and fry cummin seeds for 2
minutes.

3 Add onion and garlic and fry until golden.

4 Add garam masala, and stir well in. Fry for about 5 minutes.

5 Add drained spinach to the frying pan mixture, add a knob of ghee,
and fry gently for 5 minutes. Salt to taste. Serve.

Serves: 4

ALUR DOM
Whole Smothered Potatoes

This Kashmiri dish is a delicious way to cook new or old potatoes. No onions are used. Serve with other vegetable dishes or meat, dhal and rice.

1 lb (450 g) new potatoes
4 fl oz (115 ml) yoghurt
salt
1 teaspoon granulated sugar
½ cup corn or mustard oil
2 fresh green chillies, chopped
  (optional, or use *more!*)
water
2 tablespoons fresh chopped
  coriander or parsley

Spices
½ teaspoon coriander seeds
¾ teaspoon turmeric
½ teaspoon garam masala
2 bay leaves

SP *Spice pack available*

1 Par-boil the potatoes until about three-quarters done, then leave to cool.

2 Mix the *spices* and the yoghurt. Salt to taste, and add the sugar.

3 Prick the potatoes with a fork and dip them into the spice/yoghurt mix.

4 Heat the oil to medium then carefully place the coated potatoes into the pan. Cover, and cook until tender, about 5–10 minutes. Throw the optional chillies on top at this stage. Stir very carefully, and add water little by little to prevent it drying out.

5 Mix the fresh coriander or parsley into any remaining yoghurt, then add to the tender potatoes. Reduce heat to simmer, and serve after about 5 minutes.

Serves: 4

ALOO SIKAA HU-AA MASALADAR

Spicy Roast Potatoes

I invented these potatoes to go with a spicy turkey one Christmas.

1 lb (450 g) potatoes, peeled
   and chopped
ghee
salt to taste

Spices 1
2 teaspoons cummin seeds

Spices 2
1 teaspoon coriander, ground
1 teaspoon paprika
½ teaspoon chilli powder
   (optional)
½ teaspoon garam masala

1 Using a pan with a close-fitting lid, par-boil the potatoes until over half cooked, and drain well. Roughen the edges by placing the lid on the pan, and shaking the potatoes hard inside the pan, or scratch them over with a fork to make shallow furrows.

2 In another pan, fry *spices 1* gently in a tablespoon of ghee. Remove pan from heat and mix in the *spices 2*. Stir the potatoes into the mixture, and then transfer to the roasting pan and roast in the normal way.

3 You may need to baste them with more ghee, and sprinkle with a little salt.

Serves: 4

MATTAR PANEER
Cheese Curry with Peas

You must use fresh home-made cheese for this, which does not melt when heated. It is full of protein and easy to make. It resembles compacted cottage cheese and is very common in the sub-continent as a vegetarian dish. The only shop-bought substitute for this – paneer – is pecorino.

Cheese
4 pints (2.3 litres) gold top milk
4 tablespoons vinegar

Curry
⅓ cup ghee or oil
1 large onion, finely chopped
2 cloves garlic, finely chopped
1 inch (2.5 cm) fresh ginger, finely chopped
14 oz (400 g) tin tomatoes, mashed
1 lb (450 g) frozen peas
8 oz (225 g) of above cheese
2 tablespoons chopped fresh coriander or parsley
salt

Cheese spices
1 teaspoon cummin seeds

Curry spices
1 teaspoon coriander, ground
1 teaspoon cummin, ground
1 teaspoon turmeric
½ teaspoon chilli powder

SP **Spice pack available**

1 *To make the cheese,* boil milk, remove from heat, and add vinegar and *cheese spices.* It will separate but do *not* stir. When cool strain off whey through a tea towel into a bowl. Tie the remaining solids (the cheese) in the cloth. Put on the sink draining board and put a wooden board on top, with another weight on top of that (a heavy pan of water?) and leave standing for a minimum of 4 hours. (This compresses the cheese and squeezes out excess liquid.) Take cheese out of cloth and cut into 1 inch (2.5 cm) squares.

2 *To make the curry,* heat oil or ghee to medium to hot, and fry onion, garlic and ginger until golden. Add *curry spices* and fry mixture for 2–3 minutes on a gentle heat.

3 Add the tomatoes, simmer for 10 minutes, then add the frozen peas and simmer for a few minutes longer.

4 While this curry sauce is simmering, fry the cubes of cheese in another pan in a little ghee or oil until golden brown (or deep-fry if you prefer). Add the cheese, coriander or parsley and salt to the sauce and simmer for a further 5–10 minutes. Serve with plain rice or chupattis (page 132).

Serves: 4

ANDE MASALA
Hard-boiled Egg Curry

Hard-boiled eggs are very decorative and form an interesting addition to curries. It is traditional to add them, halved across the width, to Keema (minced meat). They also go well in seafood curries (prawn, lobster etc), and in vegetable curries (spinach, cauliflower etc) when they can be halved lengthwise. They can always appear as a garnish. Use them on pullaos and birianis in slices around the perimeter of your serving dish, or chopped and sprinkled over food, or mixed with chopped parsley or fresh coriander.
This curry should be served as a secondary dish.

6 tablespoons corn oil
2 large Spanish onions, finely
    chopped
14 oz (400 g) tin tomatoes
2 tablespoons tomato purée
salt
4–8 hard-boiled eggs
    (depending on size and
    appetite)

Spices
1 teaspoon turmeric
1 teaspoon cummin, ground
1 teaspoon garam masala
1 teaspoon coriander, ground
½ teaspoon chilli powder

1 Heat oil and fry onions until golden.
2 Mix the *spices* with water to make a paste, then add to onions. Cook for 10–15 minutes. Stir as needed.
3 Add a little water to prevent it from sticking, and then add the tomatoes and tomato purée.
4 Cook for a further 5–10 minutes, then add enough water to get the texture of sauce that you require. Salt to taste.
5 Add whole hard-boiled eggs, and cook until hot. Serve immediately.

Serves: 4

8

LENTILS, RICE & BREAD

As a source of protein, the lentil supplies almost all that meat can, is extraordinarily filling, and relatively cheap. Over 60 varieties of lentils or pulses are grown in India, and they come in all colours – red, green, yellow, white, brown, black and cream! They're round, oval, large, medium and small, split or whole, polished and with or without husk. And there are thousands of recipes containing lentils.

In the Indian sub-continent, particularly in the south, rice has become a staple food. Over the centuries, many techniques for cooking rice were developed, two paramount – biriani and pullao. Pullao is probably older than biriani, originating in the Middle East. There are numerous variations on the theme, and an equal number of spellings (*pulao, palao, pillo, pillow, pillaf*, etc). Restaurant birianis or pullaos are rarely produced in the proper way. Usually the rice is cooked separately and the fillings added and heated prior to serving. Restaurant pullaos are often coloured with artificial food colouring which, whilst attractive, is rarely authentic or even necessary.

But rice is not the natural accompaniment to curry everywhere. In a good few regions of India rice cannot grow – the climate is not wet enough – and wheat, with which to make bread, is the staple food. There is a huge range of Indian breads. Most are flat, unleavened, pancake-shaped discs, and they are baked (nan), fried (parathas), deep-fried (puris), or grilled (chupattis).

ALU CHOLE

Lentil or Chick Pea Curry

This vegetarian main-course dish is very tasty and nutritious. Serve it with nan bread or chupattis (pages oo and oo) and several fresh chutneys (see Chapter 9). It is becoming better known in the Indian restaurant.

9 oz (250 g) channa dhal, split, or whole chick peas
1 teaspoon bicarbonate of soda
1 large onion, chopped
2 tablespoons ghee
1 dessertspoon tomato purée
1 dessertspoon tomato ketchup
6–8 small potatoes, peeled and boiled
4 firm red tomatoes
salt
4 green chillies (optional)
2 tablespoons chopped fresh coriander or parsley

Spices
½ teaspoon coriander, ground
1 teaspoon cummin, ground
1 teaspoon turmeric
¼ teaspoon chilli powder
1 teaspoon mango powder
¼ teaspoon black pepper, ground
2 cloves, ground
2 bay leaves, ground
½ teaspoon pomegranate seeds, ground

SP **Spice pack available**

1 Soak the channa dhal or chick peas with the bicarbonate of soda overnight, or for a minimum of 6 hours.

2 Boil in their own volume of water, and cook until tender (about 40 minutes). If some water is not absorbed, strain and keep.

3 Fry onion in ghee until dark golden. Add *spices*, tomato purée and ketchup. Cook on medium-low heat for 5 minutes then add potatoes.

4 Combine dhal and vegetables, and cook for 5 minutes further. Add the tomatoes carefully to avoid splitting them. Add salt to taste, and a little (lentil) water if necessary.

5 Serve in a large round dish, scooping the potatoes and tomatoes to the top if you can. Garnish with chillies and/or fresh coriander or parsley.

***Serves:* 4**

MAAHN

Whole Black Lentils and Red Kidney Beans

A vegetarian meal which is packed with protein. This Punjabi delicacy is rarely, if ever, seen in Indian restaurants. It could become one of your favourites. Serve with plain rice or chupattis.

It was recognised a few years ago that red kidney beans contain toxic substances, including tannin, and in certain cases have caused quite serious illness. To remove all the toxins, you must soak the beans for 12–24 hours. During this time they swell to almost double size and discharge the toxins. Rinse before you cook them, in fresh water, and to be absolutely sure, boil during cooking for at least 10 minutes.

3 oz (75 g) red kidney beans
8 oz (225 g) whole urid (black) dhal
1½ oz (40 g) fresh ginger, finely chopped
1 tablespoon ghee or vegetable oil
1 medium onion, finely chopped
salt

Spices
½ teaspoon chilli powder
¾ teaspoon coriander, ground
1 teaspoon cummin, ground
2 teaspoons garam masala

SP *Spice pack available*

1 Soak the red kidney beans overnight for a minimum of 12 hours (see above).

2 Check through the urid dhal for grit etc, then rinse in warm water three or four times to remove dust.

3 Boil water, three times the volume of the lentils, then put in the lentils, beans and half the ginger. Boil for 10 minutes, then simmer for a further 20–25 minutes, stirring from time to time.

4 While this is going on, heat the ghee, fry the onion until golden, then add the remaining ginger and the *spices*.

5 Add this fried mix to the lentils after the 20–25 minutes of cooking, and stir well. Cook on for a further 15 minutes.

6 To test when ready mash a few lentils with back of spoon against the side of pan, and if soft, they're ready. Salt to taste. It should not be too dry (add a little water during cooking if necessary). Stir and serve at once. (If left to stand overnight it will absorb water, so add a little more while reheating.)

***Serves:** 4*

YELLOW DHAL

A very tasty accompaniment for most curries.

½ cup red lentils
salt
1 tablespoon ghee
1 small onion, chopped into
  long thin strips (optional)

Spices
1 teaspoon cummin, ground
½ teaspoon turmeric
[SP] *Spice pack available*

1 Sift through the lentils to remove grit etc, then wash them and soak them for 1 hour minimum or overnight.

2 Boil 1½ cups water, then add the lentils. Stir well.

3 After about 10 minutes, add the *spices* and salt to taste. Simmer for about 30–35 minutes. Add a little water if necessary.

4 Add 1 tablespoon ghee and when melted serve, or put into warming drawer or low oven where it will keep quite happily until you are ready.

5 If you have time and the inclination, the onion garnish makes the dhal look and taste even better. Deep-fry the onion strips until dark gold-brown in hot oil. Sieve, set aside and place on top of the dhal just before serving.

Serves: 4–6

TARKA DHAL

The most tasty of all lentil dishes and it's really easy to make.

½ cup polished moong dhal
2 tablespoons ghee
1 medium onion, finely
  chopped
1 clove garlic, finely chopped
salt
1 small onion, sliced into long
  thin strips (optional)

Spices
1 teaspoon cummin seeds
½ teaspoon black
  peppercorns (optional)
½ teaspoon turmeric

1 Sift through the lentils to remove grit etc, then wash, and soak them for 1 hour minimum or overnight.

2 Boil 1½ cups water, then add the lentils. Stir well, and cook for about 30 minutes.

3 Meanwhile fry the cummin and peppercorns in 1 tablespoon ghee for 2 minutes. Then add the onion and garlic and fry until golden.

4 Add the onion and spices mixture to the lentils when they are cooked, plus the turmeric. Add a little water if necessary, and salt.

5 Add remaining ghee and when melted serve, or put into warming drawer or low oven where it will keep quite happily.

6 If you have time, fry an onion garnish for the dhal (see page 153).

Serves: 4

Other Dhals

If you would like to experiment with more lentils and try other types, use the Yellow Dahl and Tarka Dahl recipes but use a different pulse. Try, for example, green moong dahl or channa or toor dahl. You can get these whole or split, with skins or polished. Always clean first, then soak for a few hours, cook until soft (times will vary), and spice to taste.

PLAIN BOILED RICE

I have read in many a cookbook that to cook rice properly you have to participate in all sorts of mumbo-jumbo about starch content, flavour, absorption and measuring with fingers, etc. I'm sure you can cook perfect rice with all these complicated methods, but the recipe I offer below is really simple. I have used the method hundreds of times whether cooking for a hundred or for one. It works superbly and will produce fluffy tasty rice every time.

But it is one of the few recipes in the book which requires precision timing. It is essential that you concentrate on this, and nothing else, or the rice may over-cook and become stodgy. And there's nothing worse than stodgy rice.

3 oz (75 g) rice provides a good helping per person. If you only want a small helping use 2 oz (50 g) per person.

**12 oz (350 g) Basmati or other
  long-grained rice
2 pints (a generous litre) water**

1 Pick through the rice to remove grit and particles.

2 Boil the water. It is not necessary to salt it.

3 While it is heating up rinse the rice briskly with fresh cold water until most of the starch is washed out. Run hot tap water through the rice at the final rinse. This minimises the temperature reduction of the boiling water when you put the rice into it.

4 When the water is boiling properly, put the rice into the pan. *Start timing.* (Put lid on pan until water comes back to the boil, then remove.)

5 It takes 8–10 minutes from the start. Stir frequently.

6 After about 6 minutes, taste a few grains. As soon as the centre is no longer brittle, but still has a good *al dente* bite to it, strain off the water. It should seem slightly *under*-cooked.

7 Place the strainer under the cold tap and cool the rice down. This stops it cooking further. Shake off all excess water, then place the strainer onto a dry tea towel which will help remove the last of the water.

8 After about 10 minutes, put the rice in a dish and into a low oven or warming drawer for about half an hour. As it dries, the grains will separate and become fluffy.

Serves: 4–6

PULLAO RICE
Yellow Spiced Rice

Most Indian restaurants refer to their yellow rice as Pullao Rice. Often they simply add yellow food colouring to plain rice and charge a lot more. This recipe will produce a really tasty, delicately flavoured yellow rice which is nice with most curries. It's also The Curry Club's most popular recipe.

2 cups Basmati rice
1 dessertspoon ghee
salt
¼ teaspoon saffron strands (optional)
2 tablespoons milk (optional)
pinch red food colouring powder (optional)

Spices 1
2 whole green cardamoms
2 whole cloves
2 inch (5 cm) cassia bark

Spices 2
½ teaspoon yellow food colouring powder
1 dessertspoon desiccated coconut
1 dessertspoon ground almonds

SP *Spice pack available*

1 Prepare and boil rice in usual way (see opposite).
2 Heat ghee in large frying pan or wok. Add *spices 1* and cook for about 2 minutes on medium heat.
3 Add about three-quarters of the rice, *spices 2*, and salt to taste.
4 If you want to use saffron, warm it in 2 tablespoons warm milk, let it stand for 10 minutes, stir well and add to the rice with *spices 2*.
5 Either allow to cool and reheat later (it will keep very happily for a full day), or serve at once. Just before serving mix in the remaining quarter of pre-warmed *white* rice. You'll get a nice yellow/white mixture.
6 If you want red/yellow/white, mix red food colouring powder (a pinch) with some white rice previously put aside. Allow it to stand at least 2 hours to absorb then mix it in with the white and yellow. (You can, of course, use any colouring – green, blue etc – but these are not traditional.)

Serves: *4 or more*

SHAH JAHANI PULLAO
Kashmiri Pullao

This is a festive yellow rice with lamb and peas, and the end result should be highly decorative and colourful. Arrange the ingredients as in the drawing, in wedges of peas, rice and meat, with the garnishes on top. It is a meal in itself, but you can accompany it with puris or chupattis and chutneys and pickles.

½ onion, very finely chopped
1 tablespoon corn oil
1 tablespoon tomato purée
1 lb (450 g) lean lamb in 1 inch (2.5 cm) cubes
salt
1 tablespoon chopped fresh coriander or parsley
2 cups dry Basmati rice
1 dessertspoon ghee
12 oz (350 g) peas

Spices 1
¼ teaspoon black pepper, ground
¼ teaspoon ground ginger
½ teaspoon cummin, ground
½ teaspoon paprika
½ teaspoon garam masala

Spices 2
⅛ teaspoon yellow food colouring powder
1 dessertspoon desiccated coconut
1 dessertspoon ground almonds

SP *Spice pack available*

1 For the meat, fry the onion until transparent in the oil, about 10 minutes, then lower the heat and add *spices 1*. Stir to prevent sticking and cook for 5 minutes. Add the tomato purée and fry for a further 5 minutes.

2 While the onions are frying, heat the meat in a dry, fairly hot frying pan. Stir to prevent sticking, and strain off juices as they form, straight into the onion pan. When the meat is no longer red, it's ready.

3 Add the lamb to the onion mixture, mix thoroughly, add some salt and the coriander or parsley, and cook gently for a further 20 minutes or so. The meat should be quite dry and crusty, coated in the spicy onion mixture. Keep warm.

4 Prepare and boil the rice in the usual way (see page 00), then strain.

5 When all surplus water is gone, heat rice in large frying pan or wok on medium heat. Add ghee and *spices 2* and mix in well. Cook for a further 5 minutes then put in warming drawer until you are ready to serve. Cook peas and keep warm.

6 Arrange rice, meat and peas in wedges as shown, and garnish with onion rings, deep-fried a crispy brown, chopped hard-boiled egg, a handful of almonds or pistachios, and desiccated coconut. Serve immediately to rounds of applause!

Serves: 4

VEGETABLE PULLAO RICE

A vegetarian rice dish which is delicious as either accompaniment or main dish. Vary the vegetables used if you like.

1 large onion, chopped
4 cloves garlic, chopped
1½ inch (3–4 cm) fresh ginger, chopped
ghee
½ cup peas
½ cup sweetcorn kernels
4 fresh tomatoes, chopped
1 green pepper, chopped
2 green chillies, chopped (optional)
1 large potato, peeled and very thinly sliced
2 cups Basmati rice, washed

Spices
4 cloves
2 brown cardamoms
2 inch (5 cm) cassia bark
½ teaspoon chilli powder
1 teaspoon turmeric
1 teaspoon garam masala

Garnish
chopped hard-boiled egg
chopped almonds
chopped pistachio nuts

1 Fry onion, garlic and ginger in ghee until soft. Add *spices*.
2 Add all prepared vegetables except the potato, and simmer for 5 minutes or so.
3 Meanwhile par-boil the rice. It should be slightly *under*-cooked (about 6 minutes).
4 Spread the vegetables on a flat oven dish and cover with very thinly sliced uncooked potato.
5 Cover that with the still warm rice, and cover dish with kitchen foil.
6 Cook in preheated oven at 350°F (180°C) Gas 4, for about 1 hour, then sprinkle garnish on before serving.

Serves: 4–6

PHALI PECH PULLAO

Pullao Rice with Fruit and Nuts

*This is a rich filling dish, ideal as a vegetarian main course or as a side
dish to a larger meal.*

1 small onion, finely chopped
vegetable oil
2 tablespoons sultanas
8 grapes, halved and seeded
12 × 1 inch (2.5 cm) chunks
  pineapple, fresh or tinned
2 tablespoons cashew nuts
2 tablespoons almonds,
  peeled
2 cups Basmati rice, washed
  and drained
1 small can vegetable
  consommé or ½ pint
  (300 ml) vegetable stock
salt

Spices
2 teaspoons coriander, ground
½ teaspoon black pepper,
  ground
½ teaspoon fenugreek seeds

Garnish
deep-fried onion rings
deep-fried almonds and
  cashews
hard-boiled eggs, chopped

1 Fry the onion in the oil until translucent. Add the sultanas, grapes
   and pineapple and fry for a further 10 minutes. Stir gently.

2 Add the *spices* and, after 5 minutes, the nuts.

3 Put this mixture into a heavy non-stick pan with a close-fitting lid.
   Add the rice and consommé or stock. Bring to the boil without lid.
   Stir as needed.

4 Reduce to simmer, cover and cook for 20 minutes without lifting
   lid. Check then to see whether ready. If not, cook on until rice is
   cooked.

5 Serve with garnish of onion rings, almonds and cashews and
   chopped hard-boiled eggs.

Serves: 4

NIMBU KI CHAWAL

Lemon Rice

A tasty, tangy, delicate yellow-coloured rice enhanced by curry leaves. A typical South Indian taste, which goes well with all curries.

2 cups Basmati rice
2 tablespoons ghee
2 tablespoons cashew nuts,
  skins removed, chopped
1 tablespoon fresh or
  desiccated coconut
salt
juice of 1 lime or lemon
1 tablespoon chopped fresh
  coriander

Spices
1 teaspoon mustard seeds
1 dessertspoon curry leaves
½ teaspoon turmeric

I Boil the rice in the normal way (see page 122), strain and dry out.

2 Heat the ghee and fry the mustard seeds until they pop (about 3 minutes).

3 Add the cashew nuts and curry leaves, and after a minute or so add the cooked rice and turmeric.

4 Mix well, and fry on. When hot, sprinkle on the coconut, salt to taste, and the lemon or lime juice. Serve at once, garnished with fresh coriander.

Serves: 4

NAVRATTAN RICE

One of the most decorative of rices – this is rich, looks gorgeous, and is, literally, the food of emperors. The idea is to mix three colours – orange, white and green – and place silver or gold edible foil on top.

10–12 oz (300–350 g) Basmati
   rice
1 tablespoon ghee
4 teaspoons blanched then
   deep-fried almonds, or
   other nuts
salt to taste
2 cups peas
chopped fresh coriander

Spices
4 cloves
4 green cardamoms
pinch orange food colouring
   powder
silver or gold edible foil
   (optional)

1 Wash the starch out of the rice. Boil it in plenty of boiling water for about 8–10 minutes, until slightly under-cooked (see page 122).

2 Strain and dry and divide into two halves.

3 Fry the cloves and cardamoms in the ghee for 5 minutes – do not brown them though. Add one half of the rice and mix well.

4 Take off heat, add the almonds, salt and orange food colouring powder (you want a deep orange colour).

5 Heat the peas.

6 Combine the white rice, orange rice and the green peas in a serving dish. Mix well. Place silver or gold foil and chopped fresh coriander on top. Serve immediately.

Serves: 4

BIRIANI

Birianis were developed by the inventive chefs of the Moghul emperors. The classic method of cooking them is to part-cook the rice and the filling, then to have alternate layers and filling, with a final layer of rice. Stock is poured on top, the dish is covered and sealed, and then it is baked for 45 minutes or more. It is a rich, decorative festive dish, a meal in itself. Serve with onion chutney and pickles, and a light consommé-like gravy if you like.

Use 1½ lb (675 g) of meat (chicken, beef, lamb, pork or combination), seafood (prawns, lobster, scallops or combination), or vegetables (cauliflower, carrot, courgette, aubergine, peas or combination). You could also mix meat or fish with vegetables, in a different type of combination, but always keep to the basic weight.

1 medium onion, chopped
1 large clove garlic, chopped
1 inch (2.5 cm) fresh ginger chopped
ghee
juice of ½ lemon
1½ lb (675 g) meat, seafood or vegetables (see above)
2 ripe tomatoes, peeled and finely chopped
salt

Rice
2 cups Basmati rice
¼ teaspoon saffron strands
2 tablespoons warm milk
½ small onion, chopped
½ pint (300 ml) meat stock

Spices 1
2 green cardamoms
5 black peppercorns
2 whole cloves
1 teaspoon cummin, ground
1 teaspoon coriander, ground
¼ teaspoon chilli powder

Spices 2
2 green cardamoms
2 whole cloves
2 inch (5 cm) cassia bark
2 bay leaves

Garnish
1 tablespoon sultanas
1 tablespoon halved almonds
1 hard-boiled egg, sliced

SP *Spice pack available*

1 To make the filling, fry onion, garlic and ginger in ghee until golden, then add *spices 1*. Add lemon juice, meat, seafood or vegetables, and tomatoes. If cooking meat, do so very slowly for 1 hour. Seafood requires about 30 minutes (at most), and vegetables about 15 minutes. It should all be very dry, and coated with the mix. Salt to taste.

2 Meanwhile, par-boil the rice for about 5 minutes. Strain, set aside, and soak the saffron in the milk for 10 minutes.

3 Fry the rice onion in some ghee, add the stock and saffron and milk. Add rice, heat through then strain, keeping stock.

4 Preheat oven to 325–350°F (160–180°C) Gas 3–4. Place a layer of rice (about half) in a flat dish, top with *spices 2*, then layer in filling. Top with remaining rice, pour on retained stock, cover and cook for about 1 hour. Garnish with sultanas, almonds and egg. For special occasions add pistachio nuts.

Serves: 4

KITCHEREE or KEDGEREE
Rice with Lentils

This dhal and rice mixture is a taste treat. It goes especially well with Chilli Fry (page 68). A version of kedgeree came to be adopted by the British Army messes as a breakfast food. This removed the spices and added chunks of pre-cooked haddock. It makes a delicious breakfast, and you can use this basic recipe to achieve it.

1½ cups Basmati rice	**Spices**
½ cup masoor dhal	4 cloves
1 small onion, thinly sliced	½ teaspoon black
ghee or oil	peppercorns
salt	seeds of 4 green cardamoms

1 Wash the rice and dhal together. Strain.

2 Fry onion in the ghee for about 5 minutes until soft, and then add the *spices*. Fry for a further 3 minutes, then add the rice and dhal. Fry for about 2 minutes.

3 Add 3 cups boiling water. Do not stir. Put lid on pan and simmer for 20–25 minutes.

4 Remove lid and stir rice to see whether it is fluffy. Cook further without lid if it needs it. Sprinkle salt on to taste.

Serves: 4

NAN OR NAAN
Tandoori bread

Nan bread is the traditional accompaniment to tandoori dishes. Its familiar teardrop shape is achieved because they hang inside a tandoor while cooking, and they elongate from a round shape. As most of us do not possess a tandoor this recipe uses the grill.

1 teaspoon dried yeast, or ½ oz (15 g) fresh	**Garnish**
1 lb (450 g) strong white plain bread flour	2 teaspoons sesame seeds
1 lb (450 g) white self-raising flour	1 teaspoon wild onion seeds (or more)
3½ fl oz (90–100 ml) yoghurt	

I Mash the fresh yeast in a little tepid water until it makes a runny paste. Leave in a warm place for 5–10 minutes to froth. If using dried, mix with a little sugar, and dissolve both in a little tepid water (about 15 minutes). Some new dry yeasts can be mixed directly into the flour – which is undoubtedly the easiest of all.

2 Put flours in a slightly warmed bowl, make a well in the centre, add yeast and yoghurt, and mix first with a metal spoon and then with your hands, adding more tepid water, little by little as you need it. You should have a soft, not too wet, dough that leaves the sides of the bowl clean. Knead vigorously, then put it back in the bowl, cover with a damp cloth and put in the fridge. Leave for a few hours, preferably overnight.

3 After this lengthy rising, let the dough come back to room temperature, then divide in 2 or 4 pieces (you know how much you want to eat)! Roll each piece into an oblong, or make the teardrop shape by hand. Do not roll thinner than ¼ inch (6 mm). Prick all over with a fork to prevent rising too much when cooking.

4 Preheat grill to full, and cover pan with cooking foil, shiny side up. Set grill pan shelf at half-way level.

5 Brush first piece of dough with vegetable oil on both sides, and grill one side. Turn over, sprinkle with the seeds mixture, and cook that side. It takes about 1–2 minutes per side, and darker patches develop in places. Take care not to let it burn, or to rise too much, when it will catch and burn. Cook all nans in the same way.

6 Serve and eat these nans immediately, as they do not keep well. Salt can be added at the table (I don't add salt to the dough), but they are even more delicious spread when piping hot with ghee made from butter.

Makes: 2 or 4 large nans

PESHWARI NAN

Make the nans according to the previous recipe but fold toasted sliced almonds into the centre of the dough before you roll it, and then cook in the usual way. Stud it with whole, deep-fried almonds before serving. You could also use cashew nuts.

You will need about ½ cup toasted sliced almonds, and ½ cup of deep-fried whole almonds.

CHUPATTIS

The basic Indian unleavened bread, which is very simple to make. Made without oil it is wholesome and not fattening. The spelling of chupatti (as with many words when translated phonetically) can vary – you will see chuppatti, chapati, chappatti etc.

Ata flour is the nicest to use, which you can get in most good Indian grocers (pronounced art-uh), but if you can't get it, use wholemeal or 2 parts wholemeal to 1 part white flour if you prefer a lighter dough. (You can obtain ata flour from The Curry Club.)

**8 oz (225 g) ata or wholemeal
  flour (see above)
about ¼–½ cup water**

1 Mix flour in a bowl with sufficient water to make a dough which leaves the sides of the bowl clean.
2 Take dough out of bowl and knead for a few minutes, then divide into four equal pieces.
3 Roll each one out quite thinly to about 6 inches (15 cm) in diameter.
4 Heat frying pan to very hot. Test it by touching a tiny bit of flour on the bottom of the pan. If it turns brown at once the pan is ready.
5 Using no oil, cook a chupatti on one side only.
6 Using a spatula or fish slice, take chupatti out of pan and place, uncooked side up, under a preheated grill. The top side will now cook and should puff up. Serve and eat immediately, and prepare the other chupattis similarly.

***Makes:** 4*

ROTI

Cornflour Bread (Makkhe ki Roti)

This bread comes from the North-West Frontier, now Pakistan. The first recipe uses corn or maize flour which gives it a distinctive taste. The second recipe uses besan flour instead of cornflour. They are cooked dry, like chupattis.

**8 oz (225 g) cornflour
about ¼ cup water**

1 Make a firm dough with the cornflour and water, until dough leaves side of bowl clean.
2 Divide into 6 or 8 pieces and roll into balls. Roll each out to thin discs 5–6 inches (12–15 cm) in diameter.
3 Heat frying pan, *dry* (see Chupatti recipe), and cook on one side only. Press it down with a fish slice.
4 After a minute or so, take it from the pan on the slice or spatula and place it uncooked side up under preheated grill. Grill, and the top side should puff up. Serve at once.

Makes: 6–8

Gram Flour Bread (Besan ki Roti)

8 oz (225 g) gram flour (besan)
½ cup yoghurt

1 Mix the flour and yoghurt to make a fairly firm dough. Add a little water if needed.
2 Proceed exactly as for cornflour rotis.

SRI LANKAN ROTI

This is the Sri Lankan method of making roti – a delicious fried bread with coconut.

4 oz (115 g) wholemeal or ata flour (see opposite)
4 oz (115 g) self-raising flour
2 tablespoons freshly grated or desiccated coconut
½ teaspoon salt
water
ghee or oil

1 Make a dough with the flours, coconut, salt and enough water to make a dough that leaves the side of the bowl clean. Knead it lightly then let it rest for 1 hour minimum.
2 Shape into 4–6 balls, and roll out to saucer size.
3 Shallow-fry in small amount of ghee or oil, and drain well. Serve hot.

Makes: 4–6

PARATHA

This is a larger, thicker bread and the rolling-out method should make it very light textured. It is probably the Indian version of puff pastry.

4 oz (115 g) ghee
1 lb (450 g) wholemeal or ata
** flour (see page 132)**
water
ghee or light vegetable oil,
** to fry**

1 Rub the ghee into the flour, and mix in enough water to make a dough which leaves the bowl clean. Knead for a few minutes, then leave to stand overnight (up to 24 hours).

2 The next day, divide into 4 or 6 balls, and roll each out into a thin disc. Flour it, then fold it over and over as with puff pastry. Roll out again to a thin disc. Repeat this as many times as you like – the more you do the lighter the ultimate texture. For the final time roll out to a 7–8 inch (17–20 cm) disc.

3 Melt ghee in a frying pan, to a depth of about 2 inches (5 cm). (Use a good light vegetable oil instead if you like.)

4 Fry the paratha on one side then the other, to a lovely golden brown colour. Shake off excess oil, drain on kitchen paper, and serve hot.

Makes: 4 or 6

STUFFED PARATHA

This is almost an Indian Cornish pasty or vegetable pie, but flattened and with soft 'pastry'. Serve with relishes, chutneys and pickles or, of course, as accompaniments to any Indian meal.

1 lb (450 g) wholemeal (or ata flour)

4 oz (115 g) ghee

water

ghee or light vegetable oil

Filling

2 oz (50 g) cauliflower, chopped into florets

2 oz (50 g) potato, peeled and chopped

2 oz (50 g) onion, chopped

2 oz (50 g) peas

4 fresh chillies, chopped (optional)

ghee

1 tablespoon fresh mint

salt

Spices 1

½ teaspoon chilli powder

½ teaspoon coriander, ground

½ teaspoon cummin, ground

Spices 2 (optional)

2 teaspoons roasted white cummin seeds

1 Make the paratha dough in exactly the same way as in the previous recipe (Number 1). Leave to stand overnight.

2 Simply cook the cauliflower, potato, onions, peas and chillies in a little ghee. Mash up well then add the fresh mint, *spices 1* and salt. Allow to become cold. (Make the filling at the same time as the dough and leave overnight.)

3 The next day, divide the dough into 8 or 12 balls, and roll out as described in Paratha recipe, then roll out finally into 6 inch (15 cm) discs. You need a *pair* of discs for each stuffed paratha.

4 Onto one disc lightly spread some filling. Leave an inch or 2 cm of space clear all round the edge. Brush some oil or ghee onto the other disc then press them together tightly but gently, obtaining a very good seal.

5 Roll out the sandwich carefully to about an 8 inch (20 cm) disc (sprinkling each side with some roasted white cummin seeds if you like), then deep-fry and serve as for parathas.

Makes: 4–6

PURI

These are delightful little deep-fried breads which, if made correctly, puff up like round balls. They are delicious – especially appreciated by children at tea-time – sprinkled fresh and hot with sugar. See also the Prawn Puris in Chapter 3.

**8 oz (225 g) wholemeal (or ata)
   flour
water
2 oz (50 g) ghee
oil for deep-frying**

1 Rub the ghee into the flour then mix in enough water for a dough that will leave the sides of the bowl clean. Leave to stand overnight or for a minimum of 2 hours.

2 Divide into 8 or 10 parts and roll into balls. Roll out to thin discs of around 4 inches (10 cm) in diameter.

3 Heat deep-frying oil to just below smoking point, and deep-fry each puri individually for a minute or so. Turn once in the oil and cook for a further minute. They should puff right up.

4 Shake off excess oil, drain on kitchen paper, and serve very fresh and hot.

Makes: 8–10

LOOCHEES

These are the Bengali version of puris, made with white flour instead of wholemeal. Use 8 oz (225 g) plain white flour, 2 oz (50 g) ghee and water, make dough, and fry in exactly the same way as above.

9
ACCOMPANIMENTS

Indian food usually tends to be quite rich and oil based. Fresh accompaniments – salads, chutneys, raitas and pickles – act as the perfect contrast, and aid digestion with their mouth-watering tastes.

A salad accompaniment needs minimal preparation and no cooking, and must be eaten absolutely fresh. Raitas are quick to make as well. A chutney requires more work, sometimes a little cooking, and some can be kept for a few days. Pickles require fairly long preparation and maturing times, and they keep indefinitely.

In India, the range of chutneys and pickles is much greater than you are offered in restaurants in this country, where lime, chilli, mango, onion and tandoori comprises about the whole range. This lack of imagination means, of course, that you can experiment to your heart's content at home, and I can assure you that you'll be delighted with the results.

CORN AND COCONUT SALAD

2 tender fresh cobs of corn
  (white not yellow,
  preferably)

1 cup freshly grated coconut,
  or ½ cup desiccated

½ cup chopped fresh
  coriander

juice of 2 lemons

2 (or more) chopped green
  chillies (optional)

salt and black pepper, to taste

1 Plunge the corn cobs into boiling water and boil for about 4–8 minutes (depending on freshness). Scrape the corn off the cob with a grater.

2 Combine all ingredients, add seasoning to taste, and serve chilled.

CACHUMBER SALAD

1 large onion, chopped

2 green chillies, chopped

½ green pepper, chopped

2 tomatoes, chopped

½ fresh mango, chopped

1 tablespoon chopped fresh
  coriander

1 tablespoon vinegar

1 tablespoon olive or
  sunflower oil

1 teaspoon fennel seeds

salt

Combine everything well in a bowl, adding salt to taste. Stir well prior to serving. It is sour and tasty.

GRAPEFRUIT SALAD

1 grapefruit

⅓ small onion, finely
  chopped

1 teaspoon finely chopped
  fresh coriander

1 teaspoon caster sugar

1 Peel the grapefruit, separate the segments and remove all pith and as much skin as your patience will allow, plus all pips. Catch the juice in a bowl. Do not break up the segments.

2 Mix in the other ingredients, chill and serve. As grapefruit will turn bitter if left too long, make and eat within the hour.

RADISH SALAD

10 large radishes, thinly
   sliced
1 green chilli, finely chopped

pinch mango powder
salt and ground black pepper
ice cubes

I Mix everything together 10 minutes before serving. Put into the fridge with a few ice cubes in the bowl.

2 Serve only when everything else is on the table.

RAITA

Yoghurt Chutney

A deliciously cool and cooling accompaniment. It can be varied in any of the many ways listed below. All should be chilled and served within the hour.

1 cup plain yoghurt
salt and pepper

Garnish
fresh chopped coriander
pinch of nutmeg

Spices (optional)
½ teaspoon chilli powder
½ teaspoon garam masala

I Drain any excess liquid off the yoghurt, then beat with a whisk or fork, rotary or electric beater until smooth. There should be no 'grains'.

2 Add salt and pepper plus the *spices* if used.

3 Add the other ingredients listed below at this stage to make any of the variations.

4 Serve chilled within the hour. Garnish prior to serving with fresh coriander and nutmeg.

Mixed Raita

Chop coarsely 1 inch (2.5 cm) cucumber, small onion, tomato. Add 1 tablespoon chopped fresh coriander and 1 teaspoon finely chopped fresh ginger.

Date and Raisin Raita

Chop coarsely 6 dates and 1 tablespoon raisins.

Horseradish Raita

Grate 2 inches (5 cm) fresh horseradish or use 1 dessertspoon bottled.

Mushroom Raita

Use very fresh, small white button mushrooms. Wash, dry well, and slice.

Cooked Mushroom Raita

Clean 1 cup mushrooms, slice finely. Heat 1 tablespoon mustard oil and fry ½ teaspoon each of mustard seeds and cummin seeds until they pop. Add mushrooms and cook for 1 minute. Cool before adding to yoghurt.

Mint Raita

Add 1 teaspoon finely chopped fresh mint.

Garlic Raita

Add 1 large clove finely chopped or crushed garlic.

Lemon, Orange or Grapefruit Raita

Add 1 teaspoon finely grated rind per cup yoghurt. Be careful to avoid the pith. You can combine different rinds if you like.

Cucumber Raita

Peel 2 inches (5 cm) cucumber, halve it, then cut into matchsticks.

Potato Raita

Wash, peel and boil 1 medium potato. Dice in ¼ inch (6 mm) cubes.

FRESH CORIANDER PURÉE

Any left-overs of this purée can be frozen and added to a future curry during cooking.

1 large bunch fresh coriander
1 small onion, coarsely
    chopped
2 tablespoons fresh grated
    coconut (or desiccated)

1 tablespoon lemon juice
salt

1 Take the coriander leaves off the stalks, and discard stalks.
2 Blend all ingredients in food processor or by hand.
3 Serve within 30 minutes.

FRESH CHILLI PURÉE

An excellent way of using up any spare fresh chillies. It is worth making up a large amount, as it will keep for months outside the fridge. You can add whole chillies to the purée at any time, which will become preserved, and add textural interest to the chutney. It is hot.

1 lb (450 g) fresh green chillies
1 bunch fresh coriander
    (optional)

1 large onion, coarsely
    chopped
3 tablespoons vinegar

1 Wash and de-stalk the chillies and coriander.
2 Combine all the ingredients in a food processor and grind to a purée.

FRESH CHILLI CHUTNEY

This is one for the fire eaters!

½ cup fresh green or red
   chillies
½ cup chopped fresh mint
1 tablespoon lime or lemon
   juice

1 teaspoon chopped fresh
   ginger
salt

1 Wash and dry the chillies. Cut off the stalks and chop.
2 Mix all the ingredients together about 15 minutes before serving.

VINEGARED CHILLIES

These are much less hot because the vinegar tempers the heat. Serve them with tandoori dishes.

1 cup slender fresh green or
   red chillies
1 cup (approx.) white wine
   vinegar

1 teaspoon coriander seeds

1 Wash and dry chillies, and wash and dry a screw-top coffee (or similar) jar.
2 Put the chillies and coriander seeds in the jar first, then fill with vinegar to the top.
3 Leave to stand for a week. You can start to eat them then, or leave them to mature for several months. It is essential to top up the vinegar from time to time until the chillies are well marinated.

TANDOORI CHUTNEY

This is the chutney you find in every tandoori restaurant. It is easy to make and goes well with barbecue dishes (see Chapter 4).

4 fl oz (115 ml) yoghurt
1 teaspoon chopped fresh
  mint
1 teaspoon lemon juice
  (optional)
¼ teaspoon garam masala

pinch green food colouring
  powder (optional)
pinch salt
pinch sugar

Mix everything together well, and serve.

FRESH MINT CHUTNEY

This chutney can be made in quantity when you have plenty of mint, and frozen.

½ teaspoon mustard seeds
mustard, sesame or other
  light oil
4 green chillies, chopped

pinch asafoetida
1 cup chopped fresh mint
salt

1 Fry mustard seeds in the oil until they pop, and then add the chillies and the asafoetida. Fry for a further 2 minutes.
2 Finely chop the mint and add it, with salt to taste, to the pan. Mix well, heat through briefly, then cool for at least an hour before serving.

CARROT CHUTNEY

2–3 carrots in long thin strips
6 spring onions, chopped
¼ teaspoon sugar

salt
¼ teaspoon fennel seeds
¼ teaspoon chilli powder

Mix everything together about 15 minutes before serving.

BEETROOT CHUTNEY

1 beetroot, diced
1 small onion, finely chopped
½ cup desiccated coconut
1 tablespoon chopped fresh coriander
1 tablespoon chopped fresh mint

1 teaspoon paprika
¼ teaspoon white pepper, ground
1 tablespoon lime or lemon juice
salt

1 Mix everything together about 10 minutes before serving.
2 Chill in fridge then serve.

GARLIC CHUTNEY

Here's a really potent fresh chutney for lovers of heat and garlic. Not to be consumed if you want to impress your friends the next day!

10–15 cloves garlic
2 oz (50 g) raw peanuts
½ cup desiccated, or fresh, coconut
4 green or red fresh chillies, chopped

2 teaspoons cummin, ground
juice of 1 lemon
salt
water
chilli powder

1 Put everything, except the water and chilli powder, into a blender. Use a little water as necessary to make a paste, and purée (or use a mortar and pestle).
2 Put paste into serving bowl about 1–2 hours before serving. To prevent the strong smell permeating everything, cover with foil or clingfilm.
3 Just before serving, sprinkle with chilli powder.

COCONUT AND NUT CHUTNEY

This is a rich chutney, but it goes well with many hot and sour curries such as Chilli Fry and Vindaloo.

⅓ cup desiccated, or fresh coconut, finely chopped

⅓ cup peanuts (or cashews, almonds, brazils, hazels or mixture)

⅓ cup whipped double cream

⅓–½ cup plain yoghurt

1 teaspoon coriander, ground

salt

1 Simply put everything into a blender (or pulverise by hand). The texture should be that of a loose paste.

2 Put paste into serving bowl about 1 hour before serving and garnish with something green (mint, parsley, coriander etc).

RED COCONUT CHUTNEY

Very simple to make, and looks very attractive.

½ teaspoon chilli powder (optional)

2 teaspoons paprika

¾ teaspoon salt

4 teaspoons warm top of the milk

1 cup desiccated coconut, or fresh, finely chopped

2 tablespoons lemon or lime juice (or less, to taste)

Mix the chilli powder, paprika and salt into the warm milk. Add the coconut, mix well, then add lemon juice. Serve cold.

ONION CHUTNEY

This is the restaurant standard fresh chutney. It is very easy to make.

½ onion

½ tomato

a sprig of parsley

1 teaspoon lemon juice

¼ teaspoon paprika

Finely chop onion into long strips. Cut up tomato and chop parsley. Mix together, add the lemon juice and sprinkle paprika on top.

GREEN ONION CHUTNEY

The colour looks good as a contrast to the reds, yellows, browns and whites of most Indian dishes.

- 1 large onion, finely chopped
- 1 dessertspoon chopped fresh mint and/or coriander
- 1 dessertspoon chopped spring onion leaves
- 1 teaspoon lemon juice
- pinch or drop of green food colouring

Mix everything together and serve.

TAMARIND CHUTNEY or IMLI

Traditionally served with samosas. It keeps for weeks.

- ¼–½ pint (150–300 ml) water
- 5–6 oz (150–175 g) of tamarind (about ½ packet, see page 16)
- 1 tablespoon sugar (or more to taste)
- salt
- ¼–½ teaspoon ground black pepper

1 Boil the water, and add tamarind. Work it about until it loosens. Simmer for about 20 minutes.

2 Sieve and discard the stones and husks. Add sugar, salt and pepper to the pulp. It should be quite stiff, rather like whipped cream, though not so smooth, of course. Cool for about 1 hour before serving.

GOOSEBERRY CHUTNEY

- 4 teaspoons mustard seeds
- mustard or sesame or other light oil
- 4 green chillies, chopped
- pinch asafoetida
- 4 oz (115 g) large gooseberries
- salt

I Fry the mustard seeds in the oil until they pop. Add the chillies then the asafoetida, and fry for a further 2 minutes.

2 De-seed and finely cut up the gooseberries. Add to the pan, with salt to taste. Stir and heat through briefly. Cool for at least 1 hour before serving. Eat while it is fresh.

PRAWN BALLICHOW

You will need about four 1 lb (450 g) preserving jars for this pickle, as the recipe makes rather a lot. It lasts indefinitely though.

2 pints (generous litre) vinegar

about 2 pints (generous litre) oil (or less, see method)

2 lb (900 g) prawns (thaw and dry if frozen)

4 lb (1.8 kg) small hard tomatoes, chopped

1 dessertspoon sugar

1 inch (2.5 cm) fresh ginger, finely chopped

4 cloves garlic, finely chopped

1 cup small fresh chillies

Spices 1

1 tablespoon turmeric

2 tablespoons garam masala

1½ tablespoons cummin, ground

1½ tablespoons coriander, ground

2 tablespoons paprika

1 tablespoon chilli powder (optional)

1 tablespoon mango powder

Spices 2

1 tablespoon mustard seeds

1 tablespoon cummin seeds

I Make a paste of *spices 1* and a little vinegar. Let stand for a few minutes. Meanwhile, in a cup of the oil, fry *spices 2* until they pop.

2 Add the paste to the pan and fry for 10 minutes, adding some more oil to maintain a good paste-like texture. Keep stirring.

3 Add the prawns, tomatoes, remaining vinegar and remaining ingredients – apart from the oil – and cook for 10 minutes. Preheat oven to 375°F (190°C) Gas 5.

4 Put the pickle into a casserole dish, then into the oven, and cook for 1 hour. Warm the preserving jars in or near the oven towards the end of cooking time to dry them out completely.

5 Fill the warm jars to the brim with the warm pickle, and pour over the top a liberal seal of the remaining oil.

6 Cover each jar with greaseproof paper cut to size, and cap tightly. Leave for at least 4 weeks before serving.

Makes: *about 4 lb (1.8 kg)*

BOMBAY DUCK PICKLE

For those who enjoy something fishy, this is for you. it makes an interesting alternative to crispy Bombay Duck (page 16) or Prawn Ballichow (page 147). It is not as hard to make as it may look – so do have a go...

7 oz (200 g) dry Bombay Duck
1 cup vinegar
2 cups mustard or vegetable oil
1 large onion, chopped
4 large cloves garlic, chopped
2 tablespoons tomato purée
2 tablespoons brown sugar
6 fresh green chillies, chopped (optional)

Spices 1
1 dessertspoon cummin seeds
1 dessertspoon mustard seeds

Spices 2
1 teaspoon turmeric
2 teaspoons garam masala
1 teaspoon cummin, ground
1 teaspoon coriander, ground
2 teaspoons paprika
1 teaspoon chilli powder
½ teaspoon mango powder

1   Soak the Bombay Duck overnight in the vinegar and enough water to cover.

2   Next day fry *spices 1* in half the oil until they start to pop (a few minutes only). Add the onion and garlic, and continue to cook gently.

3   Meanwhile make a paste with *spices 2* and some water. When the onion and garlic are golden (after about 10 minutes), add the spice paste. Fry about 10 minutes, stirring frequently.

4   Add the tomato purée and sugar and stir-fry for a further 5 minutes. Preheat oven to 375°F (190°C) Gas 5.

5   Put the Bombay Duck and the soaking liquid into a saucepan, bring to the boil, then simmer for 10 minutes. Strain and dispose of the liquid.

6   In an oven casserole dish, combine the duck, the fried mix and the chillies and the remaining oil. Cook in preheated oven for 1 hour.

7   Allow to cool for half an hour or so, then bottle in a preserving jar. Store for at least 1 month, after which it is ready to eat – and it will last indefinitely.

Makes: *about ½ lb (225 g)*

MEAT PICKLE

Yes, meat! I came across this ancient Punjabi recipe on a recent recipe-finding trip to India. They use goat there as the meat, but you can use any meat you like – lamb, mutton, beef, pork, chicken, turkey (goat even!). It is worth the effort to make, and I like eating it with almost any meal – Indian or otherwise.

2 lb (900 g) lean meat, skinned, boned and cubed

2 large onions, roughly chopped

8 oz (225 g) peeled garlic cloves, roughly chopped

6 oz (175 g) fresh ginger, peeled and finely chopped

½ pint (300 ml) mustard oil

1½ cups vinegar

3 tablespoons salt

4 whole green chillies

Spices

1 tablespoon cummin, ground

1 tablespoon mango powder

1 dessertspoon chilli powder

1 dessertspoon turmeric

1 dessertspoon garam masala

1 Preheat oven to 300°F (150°C) Gas 2, then dry bake the meat on oven trays for 20 minutes.

2 Meanwhile purée the onions, garlic and ginger, and heat the oil in a pan. Add the purée to the oil, and cook for 10 minutes or so.

3 Make the *spices* into a paste using some of the vinegar, and add to the onion purée. Fry for another 10 minutes.

4 Meanwhile take the meat from the oven. Strain any juices (keep for stock), and add the meat to the purée, with salt, chillies and remaining vinegar.

5 Cook for about 10 more minutes. Cool, then bottle while still warmish. Keep for 1 month before serving, and then it will last indefinitely.

Makes: *about 3 lb (1.4 kg)*

LEMON, LIME or AUBERGINE PICKLE

Lemons make an excellent substitute for limes and are much cheaper. Vary the sugar content if you prefer tarter or sweeter tastes. You can use aubergine or mango or indeed anything which takes your fancy. Just vary your times a little for softer vegetables than lemon or aubergine.

5 large lemons, 10 limes or 4 aubergines

1 teaspoon bicarbonate of soda (for lemons and limes only)

1½ pints (900 ml) vinegar

1 teaspoon salt, or more to taste

1 tablespoon sugar

1 large clove garlic, chopped finely

¾ pint (450 ml) cooking oil

4 oz (115 g) fresh green chillies (optional)

Spices

1 teaspoon turmeric

1 teaspoon cummin, ground

1 teaspoon chilli powder (or *more*)

1 teaspoon garam masala

2 teaspoons paprika

Day 1

1 For *lemons or limes*, pierce at stalk end once. Put into pan of boiling water, add bicarbonate of soda, and simmer slowly for 30 minutes. Test if skins are tender: cook a bit longer if not. Drain, remove from pan, and cut up into small pieces when cool enough. Put 1 pint (600 ml) of the vinegar, the salt and sugar into pan and bring to boil. Stir well. Add lemons and cook for 10 minutes. Put into non-metal bowl and stand overnight.

2 For *aubergines*, prepare and cook as above, but the bicarbonate of soda is not needed.

Day 2

3 Mix garlic and *spices* into a paste with some of the remaining vinegar.

4 Boil ½ pint (300 ml) oil. Remove from stove for 3 minutes before adding the spice paste. Stir over heat until the vinegar dries out and the oil comes to the surface (see Bhoona method, page 29).

5 Add lemon (or aubergine), chillies and rest of vinegar, and cook gently until the vinegar once again boils out and the oil comes to the top. Put aside to cool slightly.

6 Boil remaining oil, and lightly warm screw-top jars in oven to ensure they are dry.

7 Fill the jars with the pickle, pouring some of the hot oil on top to seal it. Cover with greaseproof paper and put on caps. Leave for at least 1 month (and it will last indefinitely).

Makes: *about 2 lb (900 g)*

MIXED VEGETABLE PICKLE

I suppose this recipe is a bit of a cheat in that you do not have to go through the huge cooking process which is the norm for pickling. I simply use my shop-bought or home-made pickles. Any vegetable-based existing pickle will do and a good dollop from several jars (your mango chutney and pickles or remnants) will combine to make a fabulous flavour. If you don't believe me, try a sample batch. It is easy to make, tastes different and nice and keeps well. I bet you'll make more.

Below I list carrots, cauliflower and sweet corn, but you can use any fresh vegetable you have to hand: potato, radish, shredded cabbage, marrow, tomato, etc. Also why not add raw cherries, raw apples, currants – anything in season? The pickle is not sweet – but fruit will enhance it.

1 cup fresh carrots, lightly blanched and chopped

1 cup cauliflower florets, lightly blanched and chopped

½ cup sweetcorn (tinned or fresh)

2 cups existing pickle (see above)

Mix everything well together and store in a screw-top jar. It can be served straightaway, and it will keep indefinitely.

Makes: *about 1 lb (450 g)*

MANGO CHUTNEY

There are dozens of different brands of mango chutney available in this country. Some are spicier than others, but on the whole they are all sweet and safe to offer to those not used to spicy food. Despite the name chutney, it really is a pickle in view of the fact that it needs longish cooking and preparation times, and it keeps for ever.

Whether some old Raj colonel did or did not invent mango chutney is not for me to say. What is for sure is that mango chutney is popularly thought to be as much a part of curry as the rice is. If you can get your hands on some fresh mangoes (and can afford them), it is easy and fun to have a go.

Jaggery (Hindi name gur) is extracted from sugar cane. The resulting juice is crystallised and dipped in molasses.

3 lb (1.4 kg) fresh firm mangoes (not too ripe)

1½ lb (675 g) brown sugar (or jaggery if you can get it)

6 oz (175 g) peeled garlic cloves, roughly chopped

6 oz (175 g) fresh ginger, peeled and finely chopped

4 oz (115 g) sultanas

4 oz (115 g) raisins

2 tablespoons salt

Spices

1 tablespoon cummin, ground

1 tablespoon coriander, ground

1 tablespoon chilli powder

1 teaspoon cloves, ground

1 Peel the mangoes and slice them, retaining all the juice.

2 Put the mango slices and juice in a little water, just enough to cover, and bring to the boil. When simmering, add the sugar (or jaggery), and extra water if necessary to prevent it sticking.

3 Purée the garlic, ginger, sultanas and raisins, and then add the *spices*.

4 When the mango acquires a jam-like consistency, add the spiced purée and the salt. Stir well and allow to simmer, adding a little more water if needed.

5 When it thickens sufficiently, take it off the heat. Cool and bottle. Leave for a minimum of 4 weeks before serving.

Makes: *about 4 lb (1.8 kg)*

GARNISHES

Indian food is very colourful and it is possible to achieve wonderful colour contrasts between white or saffron tinted rice, the browns, reds, greens and creams of the curries and the yellows of the dhals. Fresh chutneys add highlights. To top the dish you have a great creative opportunity to sprinkle on a garnish. Here are just a few ideas – have fun thinking up more of your own.

fresh chopped parsley or coriander

blanched or fried whole almonds

strips of ginger, raw or deep-fried

red or green pepper strips

green chilli, sliced

grilled tomato slices

boiled beetroot strips

cucumber dipped in egg white and fried

hard-boiled egg, crumbled or sliced

deep-fried parsley sprigs

deep-fried coriander leaves

deep-fried red cabbage strips

chopped chives

grilled or sautéed mushrooms, thinly sliced

small fried whole mushrooms

onion rings, fried crispy brown

roasted red chilli strips

batter-fried slices of lime or lemon

raisins

sultanas

desiccated or grated coconut

10
SWEETS, DESSERTS & BEVERAGES

India probably cooks the spiciest food on earth and
to counter it she is also responsible for the sweetest
sweets. To Western tastes they are far too sweet and
rich at first, but they are delicious once one becomes
used to them. As with all aspects of Indian cuisine,
there is an enormous range of sweets from all parts
of the sub-continent, but for reasons known only to
themselves, only a handful of Indian restaurants
offer Indian desserts and sweets on their menus. You
can, of course, always serve fresh fruit, but here I
offer you a limited selection of the many delights
that can end your Indian feasts.

I also include some drink recipes. Cold beverages
are very popular in India – lhassi and fresh lime
being the favourites – and restaurants are beginning
to offer them over here. They are simple to make
and you are likely to become hooked. For other ideas
on what to drink with your meal, see Chapter 1. I
also include some tea recipes – of course!

BARFI or BURFI
Indian Fudge

Barfis are very more-ish – you'll want more once you try them! There are variations involving pistachios, coconut etc, but this recipe is for plain barfi. Simply add any nuts and/or coconut if you want to make a change, and green, orange, red, pink, or yellow food colouring to obtain effects. Traditionally barfi is made by reducing milk to a solid by stirring for hours over the stove (koya). I use dried milk powder, which saves a lot of time.

Both kewra *and* vark *are available from The Curry Club Mail Order Service.*

6 oz (175 g) sugar (more if you have a sweet tooth)

1 cup water

8 oz (225 g) dried milk powder (or full cream milk powder)

1 dessertspoon ground almonds

½ teaspoon green cardamom, ground

½ teaspoon rosewater or kewra

edible silver or gold leaf (vark) (optional)

1 Slowly boil the sugar and water to a stiffish syrup.

2 Stir in, still on gentle heat, the milk powder, almonds, cardamom and rosewater.

3 Mix well and when quite thick remove from heat and turn out into a non-stick oven dish (approx. 10 × 8 inches/25 × 20 cm).

4 When cold and set, turn out of the dish. Place edible foil on it (optional), then cut into fudge-sized pieces. Keep for 4 days only.

GAJAR HALWA
Carrot Fudge

The idea of sweets made from carrots is an intriguing one. It is an unlikely sounding combination which gives a delicious result. I warn you now that you need at least a free afternoon in which to make this recipe. So it's for the dedicated only...

1¼ lb (500 g) good fresh carrots, scrubbed and finely grated

1¾ pints (1 litre) milk

5 oz (150 g) sugar

4 tablespoons ghee

a few drops rosewater essence

1 teaspoon cardamom, ground

1 oz (25 g) each almonds, pistachios, raisins

4 dried dates, or fresh (see below)

1 Place finely grated carrots into a pan with the milk and cook over a medium heat until the mixture turns dry and thick. This will take about 1–1½ hours. Stir all the time, and watch carefully. When you can pull the mixture away from the bottom of the pan easily, with no liquid running, it is ready.

2 Add the sugar and stir until sugar is dissolved and absorbed. Adding the sugar will make the mixture runny again so you should expect to spend 20–30 minutes on this.

3 Add 4 tablespoons pure ghee and fry until it goes a pleasant dark orange-brown colour.

4 Mix in the rosewater essence and ground cardamom.

5 Leave to set in a shallow greased baking tin, or on a large plate. If you set it in the fridge overnight it becomes rather like fudge.

6 Turn it out onto a dish, cut into squares and decorate with the chopped nuts and fruit. You will need to soak the dried dates in cold water first – or use fresh ones if you can.

Serves: 4–6

Sujee halwA

Semolina Fudge

This is a recipe my grandmother brought back from India. Serve cold.

3 oz (75 g) semolina
2 cups water
3 oz (75 g) white sugar
pinch of salt
1 dessertspoon sultanas, fried in ghee
1 dessertspoon chopped walnuts

black seeds of a cardamom, or ½ teaspoon ground cardamom
1 level tablespoon grated fresh or desiccated coconut (optional)
2 oz (50 g) butter

1 Put the semolina into a dry pan, and cook over a medium heat until golden brown. Take care not to let it burn – it 'turns' quite fast. It takes about 10 minutes. Put the pan to one side.

2 Boil the water in another pan, and add the sugar, salt, sultanas, walnuts, cardamom and coconut. Turn the heat down to a simmer then stir the mixture to blend it.

3 Add the butter and slowly sprinkle in the semolina, stirring all the time.

4 The mixture will gradually thicken. When it is completely blended and the consistency of soft mashed potato, turn it out into a serving dish. Decorate and chill before serving – on special occasions with whipped cream.

Serves: 4

KULKULS

This recipe is for decorative sweets which are ideal for a party or as petit fours with coffee. You can make them the day before.

12 oz (350 g) plain white flour
4 oz (115 g) rice flour
pinch of salt
2 oz (50 g) butter
3 oz (75 g) desiccated coconut

about 7 fl oz (200 ml) milk
2 eggs
icing made from icing sugar and water
oil for deep-frying

1 Mix flours and salt in a bowl and rub in the butter.

2 Boil the coconut in the milk. Remove from heat and leave to stand for 15 minutes. Strain the milk and keep the coconut to one side.

3 Add the milk to the eggs in a bowl and beat until well mixed.

4 Add the milk/egg mixture and the moist coconut to the flour and knead into a pliable dough.

5 Take a walnut-sized piece of dough, roll it into a ball and press it into the back of a fork. Roll the dough off the fork by putting the loaded side of the fork onto the work surface and pulling the fork forward to release the dough into a rolled-up 'shell'. Shape all the dough in this way.

6 Deep-fry the shells in fairly hot oil (not smoking hot), until light golden brown. Drain well, allow to cool, and then coat with icing. Allow icing to set before serving. Keep for 4 days only.

Makes: 20–30

LADDU

Sweet Lentils Balls

Laddus are sweet golf-ball-sized balls which can be made from all sorts of ingredients. This recipe uses green moong dhal as its base.

1 lb (450 g) green moong dhal
½ pint (300 ml) water
1 lb (450 g) brown sugar
8 oz (225 g) dried milk powder
½ teaspoon green cardamom seeds, ground

2 oz (50 g) mixed nuts, chopped
¼ teaspoon green food colouring powder
desiccated coconut
knob of ghee

1 Pick through the dhal to remove grit. Wash it, then dry in a moderately warm oven. Grind to flour in a coffee grinder (see page 14).

2 Make a syrup by boiling the water, adding sugar, and stirring often until you get a thick syrup (5–10 minutes).

3 Mix the dhal flour with the milk powder, cardamom powder, nuts and green colouring. Mix it all into the syrup to obtain a stiff sticky mixture. Keep on low heat and keep stirring. Add a knob of ghee.

4 Spoon out some mixture and roll into golf balls, rolling in the coconut as you go.

5 Keep the mixture on a low heat and stir often until it is all used up. Allow the balls to cool, then serve. Keep for 4 days only.

Makes: 8–10

BANANA FRITTERS

If you've not had banana fritters, you've not lived! Get into the kitchen and try this recipe at once. You'll find it to be a fantastic treat, which is typical of the type of recipe invented by the British in India during the Raj. This particular recipe was written down by my grandmother in 1902 in Agra.

1 egg	5 fl oz (150 ml) milk (approx.)
pinch of salt	3 bananas
1 teaspoon sugar	ghee
1 tablespoon flour	caster sugar

1 Beat egg with pinch of salt and sugar, and fold in flour and milk to make a batter.

2 Finely cut up the bananas and add to the batter.

3 Heat a tablespoon of ghee in the frying pan, then add a dessertspoon of batter at a time, to make 3 inch (7.5 cm) fritters. When golden brown on one side, turn over. Drain on kitchen paper and keep warm.

4 When all fritters are done sieve caster sugar gently on top of them. Serve hot.

Makes: *16 fritters*

JALEBI

Everyone knows jalebi – those curly golden spirals of batter immersed in sticky syrup – but how many know how to make them? The truth is it takes a bit of practice, and a bit of time. If you love jalebis keep trying, then – hey presto – it's easy, isn't it! They can be served hot or cold.

8 oz (225 g) plain flour	½ teaspoon kewra or
2 tablespoons plain yoghurt	rosewater
½ oz (15 g) saffron strands	oil for deep-frying
½ pint (300 ml) water	2 tablespoons chopped
8 oz (225 g) white sugar	pistachio nuts (optional)

Day 1

1 Combine the flour, yoghurt and a little extra warm water to make a thickish batter. Add the saffron and put the batter in a warm place (the airing cupboard?) for a maximum of 24 hours, a minimum of 12. This allows the yoghurt to ferment.

2 At the same time make the syrup by boiling the ½ pint (300 ml) water then adding the sugar. Boil for about 10 minutes, stirring often. Take off heat when you get quite a thick syrup. Add the rosewater. Stand syrup to cool for the same length of time as the batter.

Day 2

3 Stir the batter well. Add a little warm water if needed but keep it quite thick. Preheat the oil for deep-frying to fairly hot.

4 Now here's the tricky bit. You've got to get the batter into the deep-frying oil in a controllable thin spiral. Fill a large plastic bag with the batter. Grasp it firmly then lift one corner away from the batter and snip a *tiny* hole in the bag by cutting off the corner with a pair of scissors. The hole should be smaller than pencil size.

5 Now simply squirt the batter into the hot oil in squiggles and figure-eights. The correct size for each jalebi is about 3–4 inches (7–10 cm) in diameter, but don't worry if yours are bigger or smaller. To stop pouring, lift the corner up and away.

6 Do not over-cook them, and turn them over once. When golden on both sides, remove from oil, drain well and plunge straight into the cold syrup in a nearby bowl or dish.

7 Soak them in the syrup for a maximum of 5 minutes, then sprinkle with pistachios before serving if you like.

Makes: *8–10*

Lagun nu custard

This recipe was given to me by the Executive Chef of the Searock Hotel in Bombay, which is one of the city's best-known eating places. I found it particularly delicious cold, when it sets like a firm milk pudding.

1 pint (600 ml) milk
3 oz (75 g) sugar
3 eggs, separated
5 fl oz (150 ml) double cream

few drops rosewater essence
chopped nuts and a little ground cardamom for topping

1 Boil milk with sugar over a low heat, stirring all the time, until it reduces to about one-third of its original volume.
2 Take off the heat and allow to cool. Beat the egg yolks and whites separately.
3 Add the cream, yolks and rosewater to the milk and beat the mixture until well blended. Fold in the whipped egg whites.
4 Pour into a greased baking dish and bake in a hot oven for half an hour at 425°F (220°C) Gas 7.
5 Decorate with nuts etc, and serve hot or chilled.

Serves: 4

Kulfi
Indian Ice Cream

Ice cream has been made in India for centuries. Legend has it that the Moghul emperors used to send runners up into the Himalayas to carry back huge chunks of ice, which were no more than ice-cube size when they reached the palaces in the plains. Be that as it may, Kulfi remains a favourite Indian dessert. It is firmer and sweeter than its Western counterpart.

8 oz (225 g) tin condensed
   milk
¾ pint (450 ml) double cream
2 oz (50 g) sugar
3 drops vanilla essence

2 oz (50 g) pistachio nuts,
   chopped (optional)
2 oz (50 g) almonds, chopped
   (optional)

1 Heat milk and cream to boiling point, then add the sugar.
2 Simmer for about 15 minutes, stirring often. Add the vanilla essence about half-way through.
3 The mixture will reduce and thicken, which is the time to add the nuts if you are using them.
4 Turn into a suitable container and freeze. Leave at least 24 hours before serving.

Serves: 3–4

MANGO MOUSSE

This is one of those recipes beloved by the British community in India. It makes a delightful dessert and goes well after an Indian main course.

1 packet lemon or lime jelly
1 pint (600 ml) boiling water
1 fl oz (25 ml) lime juice
grated rind of 1 lemon

8 fl oz (225 ml) double cream
1 large tin Alfonso mangoes,
   drained and chopped
1 egg white

1 Chop up the jelly and add to the boiling water, along with the lime juice and lemon rind. Set aside to cool, but not to set.
2 Whip the cream, then add the chopped mangoes.
3 Continue whipping, then add the jelly.
4 Whisk the egg white and fold into the other ingredients. Leave to set in fridge.

Serves: 3–4

GULAB JAMAN

If you like Indian sweets you'll like Gulab Jaman. And you'll know it well, as it is a regular star on the Indian restaurant menu. It consists of cake-like balls immersed in syrup and served cold.

1 tablespoon plain flour	½ pint (300 ml) water
6 oz (175 g) dried milk powder	6 oz (175 g) sugar
1 tablespoon yoghurt	½ teaspoon kewra or
1 tablespoon ground almonds	rosewater
½ teaspoon ground	oil for deep-frying
cardamom	

1 Mix the flour, milk powder, yoghurt, ground almonds and cardamom, using a little extra water as necessary to achieve a stiff dough. Leave to stand for 2 hours minimum, then form into 8 balls.

2 Boil the ½ pint (300 ml) water, add the sugar, and simmer until you get a thickish syrup. Add the rosewater.

3 Preheat the oil for deep-frying. (Ghee is the best for flavour, but a good vegetable oil will do.) Keep at a medium heat.

4 Fry the balls for at least 5 minutes. They need to cook right through – the outside should be brown/gold, while inside is a creamy colour. When cooked, shake off excess oil, cool a bit, then steep them in the warm syrup.

5 Chill in the fridge until ready to serve.

Makes: 8

RASGULLAS

Cream Cheese Balls in Syrup

These look rather similar to Gulab Jaman, being small balls in syrup. In this case they are pale coloured and made from paneer (cream cheese). Make the cheese yourself, and I warn you, the pudding is very sweet.

1 recipe Paneer (see page 114)	½ pint (300 ml) water
1 tablespoon semolina	6 oz (175 g) sugar
1 teaspoon cornflour	1 teaspoon rosewater or
1 teaspoon ground almonds	kewra

1 Make the cheese the day before as described in cheese recipe.

2 Mix the semolina, cornflour and ground almonds with the cheese to make a pliable dough. Form into golf-ball-sized balls, about 8 in all.

3 To make the syrup, boil the water, add the sugar, and stir over gentle heat until it thickens. Gently put the balls into the syrup and simmer for 15 minutes.

4 Take off the heat and cool. Place in serving bowl, and sprinkle on the rosewater. Put into fridge for 12 hours minimum before serving. Serve within 48 hours.

Makes: *about 8*

RASMALAI
Cream Balls

This is a richer version of Rasgulla. In this case the rasgulla is given a filling and cream (malai) is added.

Rasgulla ingredients, as previous recipe
3 tablespoons chopped mixed nuts
½ pint (300 ml) double cream
1 small tin sweetened condensed milk
½ cup water
⅛ teaspoon yellow food colouring powder

1 Make the rasgullas as in previous recipe, but do not chill.

2 Remove them from the syrup, and flatten them to round rissole shapes.

3 With your thumb, make an indentation in the centre, then fill it with a small quantity of the chopped nuts. 'Bury' the nuts inside by squeezing the indentation flat, but keeping the basic rissole shape.

4 Mix the cream, condensed milk, water and food colouring powder with the existing syrup, then place the balls in it.

5 Place in the fridge and chill for 12 hours minimum before serving. Serve within 48 hours.

Makes: *about 8*

Sweet mincemeat samosas

It wasn't until Victorian times that traditional savoury mincemeat gave way to the sweet version we know today. Here I've gone a stage further, and taken a light, fresh mincemeat recipe and spiced it up to make an alternative samosa suitable for a spicier Christmas.

14 oz (400 g) fresh (ready-made, frozen or home-made) puff pastry

egg white for sealing and glazing

Filling

4 oz (115 g) Cox's apples, peeled, cored and chopped small

10 oz (300 g) mixed dried fruit (sultanas, raisins, currants)

½ oz (15 g) mixed peel, very finely chopped

4 oz (115 g) grapes (black or green), peeled, seeded and chopped

4 oz (115 g) chopped mixed nuts

3 oz (75 g) caster sugar

juice and rind of ½ small lemon

1 teaspoon melted butter or ghee

dash of sweet sherry

1 teaspoon ground almonds

Spices

½ teaspoon ground cloves

½ teaspoon ground cassia bark

½ teaspoon mixed spice

1 teaspoon fennel seeds, lightly toasted

1 For the filling, mix all the ingredients and *spices* together.

2 Roll out the puff pastry, keeping the oblong shape if you've used frozen or ready-made (*make* it oblong in shape if you've made your own). Cut into quarters, then cut each portion again into four, and roll any sections that need it into as near a square as you can get.

3 To make the samosas, brush two edges of a square with egg white. Place 2 teaspoons of filling onto the square and fold one corner to its diagonal opposite. Seal well. Brush with egg white. Repeat until all pastry squares are used up.

4 Bake in a preheated oven at 450°F (230°C) Gas 8, for 10–15 minutes until pastry has risen and is golden. Serve as finger foods with drinks or with whipped cream as a dessert. I prefer them hot.

Makes: 16

SPICY FRUIT SALAD

Fruit responds remarkably well to savoury spicing and is deliciously refreshing as a dessert. It's really easy to make, so try it and see. Any fruit in season can be used; the following list is just a suggestion of the varieties that can happily mix together.

1 orange
1 grapefruit
1 apple
2 bananas
1 pear
20 red cherries
1 cup blackberries
1 small tin mangoes, or 1
  large fresh mango
6 ice cubes
1 teaspoon chopped fresh
  mint

Spices
1 tablespoon white sugar
1 teaspoon salt
1 teaspoon ground black
  pepper
¼ teaspoon ground ginger

1 Prepare – peel, core, de-pip, whatever – the fruit, then chop it up if necessary to approximately the same size pieces. Mix together well so that the pear and apples pieces don't discolour.

2 Mix the *spice* ingredients together.

3 About 20 minutes before serving mix the fruit and the ice cubes. Sprinkle the spices over the fruit, and garnish with the mint leaves. Keep in the fridge until you serve.

Serves: 4–6

TEA

Tea is one of the major exports from India and Sri Lanka. There are a number of well-known Indian species. Darjeeling grows at the foot of the Himalayas and is known as the 'champagne of teas' because of its delicate 'muscatel' flavour and its fine bouquet. Assam grows in profusion in the north-east of India, and is India's most prolific tea. It is strong flavoured and was the first Indian tea to be discovered, in 1823, by a Briton. Nilgiri tea grows in the south of India. It is regarded as a connoisseur's tea with a fine strong flavour. Other varieties growing in India are hybrids including some Chinese/Indian combinations.

Sri Lanka has been a tea producer since 1870. Two main teas are produced in the Dimbula and Ura districts, and flavours range from delicately perfumed to strong.

The British are the world's greatest tea-drinkers, consuming an average of 1,650 cups a year per head. In these days of blended tea bags, it is easy to forget how good tea is and how versatile it can be. Here are some hints on how to produce a really good cup of tea, as well as a few of my tea variations in the following pages.

1 Use only freshly poured tap water from the cold tap. This ensures maximum oxygen in the water.
2 Boil more water than you need.
3 Pre-warm the teapot while the kettle boils (use the hot tap).
4 As the kettle comes to the boil, empty the teapot of hot tap water and put in your tea.
5 The minimum is one teaspoon or tea bag per cup plus one or two 'for the pot' if you like it stronger.
6 Add boiling water. Put any spare in the cups to warm them.
7 Allow the tea to stand in the teapot brewing for 3–5 minutes, then empty the cups just before serving.

ICED TEA

There is nothing more refreshing on a hot summer's day than iced tea. Try this slightly spicy one for a change.

Per glass

tea	**sugar (optional)**
2 green cardamoms	**sprig of mint**
ice cubes	**slice of lemon**

I Prepare tea in the usual way (see previous page). A fragrant tea such as Darjeeling is better than a strong one.

2 Allow the pot to brew for about 5 minutes. Add 2 green cardamoms (split open) per person.

3 Pour the tea into a jug using a strainer and let it cool down (for at least 10 minutes).

4 Three-quarters fill a tumbler with ice cubes. Top up with the cool tea. Add sugar if required and garnish with a sprig of mint and a slice of lemon. Drink through a straw.

ICED TEA COCKTAIL

This sounds fiddly to make but it is quite simple really. You can vary the fruit juices if you wish but stick with the lemon juice, tea, soda, and at least two sweeter juices. Use a rounded bottom ½ pint (300 ml) stemmed glass.

Per glass

3 ice cubes

1 tablespoon rosehip syrup

1 tablespoon fresh lemon juice

1 tablespoon sugar syrup (sugar and water dissolved)

1 tablespoon pineapple juice

1 tablespoon orange juice

soda water

cold tea

slice of orange and lemon

2 bottled cherries

I Put the ice cubes into the glass and a straw as well at this stage.

2 Pour in the rosehip syrup, then very carefully add the further ingredients one by one. If you do it very slowly you will get each juice sitting above the next in a sort of layering effect which looks stunning. Top up with soda and cold tea. Do not stir. Leave that to the drinker.

3 Garnish with a slice of orange and lemon, and a couple of bottled cherries.

KHAVA
Kashmiri Tea

Ever thought of spicing tea? The Indians have. They add anything from peppers to mint. This recipe comes from Kashmir at the foot of the Himalayas, and is very fragrant.

Per cup

tea leaves or tea bag (as normal)
2 almonds, halved

2 green cardamoms, split
1 inch (2.5 cm) cassia bark

1 Prepare ingredients for the number of cups you wish to serve.
2 Put the right number of full cupfuls of cold water into a saucepan and add the ingredients.
3 Bring to the boil and then simmer for 3 minutes.
4 Sieve the liquid into your teapot, and discard the ingredients. Serve with or without milk.

CINNAMON TEA

The Indian alternative to lemon tea. It is quite delicious and looks very attractive in a glass.

Per cup

tea leaves or tea bag (as normal)
½ teaspoon fennel seeds

2 inch (5 cm) cassia bark
1 cinnamon stick

1 Make tea as you normally do, using a fragrant delicate tea like Assam.
2 Add to the teapot the fennel seeds and cassia bark.
3 Brew as usual, and serve in a glass, straining as you pour. Use no milk, and add a cinnamon stick to each glass to decorate.

JEERA PANI
Cummin Water

This is a cool drink to try on a hot afternoon in place of tomato juice or as an appetiser. It can be drunk as it is (and quite delicious it is too), or it can be added to tomato juice.

½ cup lemon juice or PLJ
1 tablespoon white wine
    vinegar
1 teaspoon Worcestershire
    sauce
½ teaspoon sugar
½ teaspoon salt
1 pint (600 ml) water
½ pint (300 ml) crushed ice

Spices
1 tablespoon cummin, ground
1 teaspoon garam masala
1 teaspoon paprika
½ teaspoon chilli powder
    (optional)

1   Mix all the ingredients together except the water and ice, and let stand for 10 minutes.
2   Add the water, sieve off the husks and lemon pips etc, and serve with the ice.

JAL JEERA

This is a simpler version of the previous recipe.

1 pint (600 ml) water
1 teaspoon chopped fresh
    mint
1 teaspoon salt, or to taste
sugar (optional)
½ pint (300 ml) crushed ice
    (optional)

Spices
1 tablespoon tamarind juice
    (see page 00) or 1 teaspoon
    brown sugar +1 tablespoon
    vinegar
1 teaspoon cummin, ground
½ teaspoon chilli powder

1   Mix all the ingredients together, and let stand for at least 10 minutes to ensure that all the ingredients and flavours blend.
2   Serve cold with crushed ice, or heat all through in a pan.

SPICY TOMATO JUICE

Quick and simple, this can be served icy cold or piping hot!

2 pints (generous litre) tomato
  juice
1 teaspoon Worcestershire
  sauce
½ teaspoon Tabasco sauce
juice of ½ lemon
½ pint (300 ml) crushed ice
salt

Spices
pinch (less than ⅛ teaspoon)
  garam masala

1   Combine all the ingredients, stir well, and serve at once.

2   You could, if you like, add a measure of vodka, aquavit, kirsch or other white spirit alcohol. It makes a *wonderful* Bloody Mary!

LHASSI NAMKEEN

A savoury yoghurt drink. Served cold, this is a traditional Indian beverage to accompany a curry, and it is becoming popular in Indian restaurants over here.

8 fl oz (225 ml) plain yoghurt
1 pint (600 ml) water
4 ice cubes

½ teaspoon ground white
  pepper
salt to taste

Simply put everything in a blender, and blend together. Serve with more ice cubes if you wish.

LHASSI MEETHI

The sweet version of Lhassi, which is equally delicious with curry. Serve icy cold.

½ pint (300 ml) plain yoghurt
½ pint (300 ml) milk
1 pint (600 ml) water

4 drops rosewater
3 teaspoons sugar
½ pint (300 ml) crushed ice

Put all the ingredients except the ice into a blender, and blend about 1 minute at high speed. Add crushed ice, and serve in glasses.

Fruit Lhassi

Follow the instructions for Lhassi Meethi. Add any fruit of your choice, about 2–3 oz (50–75 g), before blending if you want it smooth, or after blending if you want a texture.

NIMBU

Nimbu means lime in Hindi, and they grow prolifically in India (lemons are rare). One of the uses of the lime is to produce a truly refreshing and delicious cold drink, which comes in four versions – sweet or 'sour', or with soda or plain water. In this country, use limes if you can get them (and can afford them) – or use fresh lemons, bottled pure lemon juice or PLJ.

Dilute the lemon juice in the glass with as much water or soda as you would ordinary squash.

4 lemons (or more if you like
    it strong)
2–3 ice cubes

1 Squeeze the lemons and crush the ice.
2 For *Nimbu Pani*, add water to the lemon juice in a glass.
3 For *Nimbu Soda*, add soda instead of water to the lemon juice.
4 For *Nimbu Namkeen*, ('sour' or more specifically 'salty'), add salt and pepper to either the water version or the soda version.
5 For *Nimbu Meethi* (sweet), add sugar to taste to the water or soda version.

SHARBAT

This is a cold fruit drink. You can use any fruit of your choice – blackcurrants, blackberries, raspberries, strawberries, mango, pineapple, peaches or apricots.

1 lb (450 g) fruit, skinned if necessary
1½ pints (900 ml) water

¼ pint (150 ml) crushed ice
sugar to taste

1 Mash the fruit, then add the water. Stand for a minimum of 6 hours.

2 Strain, and serve with the crushed ice. Add sugar to personal taste.

Makes: 2 pints (generous litre)

APPENDIX 1

The Curry Club is all about curry. Whether your interest is cooking or dining out The Curry Club is dedicated to bringing you all you need to enhance your enjoyment of that extraordinary food.

Founded in January 1982 by Pat Chapman and Fiona Ross it now has many thousands of members throughout the UK and world-wide. Members receive a bright and colourful quarterly magazine which has regular features on curry and the curry lands. *The Curry Magazine* is produced on art paper and keeps members in touch with everything to do with curry. Original recipes appear, sometimes with photographs, from all countries which enjoy authentic curries – from India, Pakistan, Bangladesh, Nepal, Burma, Sri Lanka and further afield, from Singapore, Malaysia, Thailand, even China occasionally. Features about the history and culture of these fascinating lands back up the food side, and members regularly contribute by writing of their experiences. Readers' letters and members' reports on restaurants, 'Restaurant Roundup', are popular features. We write about spices and review curry cookery books and have some lighthearted pages with a crossword and puzzles, cartoons and sometimes stories and there's even a gossip column which keeps tabs on what the manufacturers and popular personalities are up to – and it's all curry, of course.

The Curry Club publishes *The Good Curry Guide* annually. It is a critical study of Indian-style restaurants throughout the country. Did you know there are over 3,000 Indian restaurants in the UK? Where are the best of these? The *Guide* lists and describes well over 1,000 plus a listing of overseas restaurants world-wide. It also contains feature and background articles by well-known writers. We also operate a discount scheme for members at restaurants.

The Curry Club also runs a highly acclaimed and efficient mail order service. Over 200 items are stocked including whole spices, ground spices, pickles, pastes, dry foods, tinned food, joss sticks, gift packs and a full range of Indian cookbooks by other authors. We also offer a range of forty packs of pre-mixed spices which make dishes for four and, as well as removing the chore of mixing the spices, assists you in getting to know about them. Where one of these forty recipes appears in this book, the spice list is marked SP *Spice pack available*

On the social side the Club organises regular activities all over the UK. These range from a regular monthly club night in London and club nights from time to time elsewhere, enabling members to meet the Club organisers, discuss specific queries, buy supplies and enjoy curry snacks and meals, usually in the private function room of a pub or similar location. We also hold day and residential weekend cookery courses, gourmet nights to selected restaurants and similar enjoyable outings.

Top of the list is our regular Curry Club Gourmet Trip to India. We take a small group of curry enthusiasts, including ourselves, to India and tour the incredible sights all over the country in between sampling the foods of each region.

If you'd like to know more write to:
The Curry Club, Freepost, Haslemere, Surrey GU27 1BR.
Telephone: 0428 2452

APPENDIX 2

The Store Cupboard

There are well over sixty main spices and dried herbs in common use in Indian cookery. In addition there are over sixty pulse types, dozens of rices, nuts and dry foods which you could use to cook Indian.

I've simplified this to a workable list of items you need in your store cupboard to make the recipes in this book, and of these, I have sub-divided them into essential and non-essential. The essential items appear again and again in the recipes, the non-essential appear only in one or two.

Before you start cooking check your stores. Nothing guarantees putting you off a cookbook better than finding you don't have an ingredient. This list may look a bit formidable but remember once you have the items in stock they will last for some time. And again I have listed in metric only as most of the packaging these days *is* metric only.

All the items listed are available in the quantities stated, by post from The Curry Club.

ESSENTIAL WHOLE SPICES	SUGGESTED QUANTITY
Bay leaves	10 g
Cardamom, black or brown	50 g
Cardamom, green or white	50 g
Cassia bark	50 g
Chillies	50 g

ESSENTIAL WHOLE SPICES	SUGGESTED QUANTITY
Cloves	50 g
Coriander seeds	100 g
Cummin seeds, white	100 g
Curry leaves, dry	10 g
Fennel seeds	100 g
Fenugreek leaves, dry	50 g
Mustard seeds	100 g
Peppercorns, black	100 g
Sesame seeds	100 g
Wild onion seeds	100 g

ESSENTIAL GROUND SPICES

Black pepper	100 g
Chilli powder	100 g
Coriander	100 g
Cummin	100 g
Garam masala	100 g
Garlic powder	100 g
Ginger	100 g
Paprika	100 g
Turmeric	100 g

NON-ESSENTIAL WHOLE SPICES

Alkenet root	25 g
Cinnamon bark	100 g
Cummin seeds, black	100 g
Dill seeds	100 g
Fenugreek seeds	100 g
Ginger, dried	100 g
Lovage seeds	100 g
Mace	100 g
Nutmeg, whole	50 g
Panch phoran	25 g
Pomegranate seeds	50 g
Poppy seeds	100 g
Saffron stamens	½ g

NON-ESSENTIAL GROUND SPICES	SUGGESTED QUANTITY
Asafoetida	50 g
Cardamom, green	25 g
Cassia bark	25 g
Cloves	25 g
Mango powder	100 g

ESSENTIAL DRY FOODS

Basmati rice	2 kg
Desiccated coconut	100 g
Gram flour	1 kg
Masoor (red) lentils	500 g

NON-ESSENTIAL DRY FOODS

Bombay duck	200 g
Food colouring powder, red	25 g
Food colouring powder, yellow	25 g
Lentils – Channa, split	500 g
Moong green, whole	500 g
Toor or tovar, split	500 g
Urid, whole black	500 g
Nuts – Almond, whole	50 g
Almond, ground	100 g
Cashew	100 g
Peanuts, raw	100 g
Pistachio	100 g
Papadams, spiced and plain (pack)	300 g
Puffed rice (*mamra*)	500 g
Red kidney beans	500 g
Rice flour	500 g
Rosewater, bottle	7 fl oz
Sev (gram flour savoury)	200 g
Silver leaf (edible)	6 sheets
Supari mixture	100 g
Tamarind block	400 g

GLOSSARY

A

Achar   Pickle

Adrak   Ginger

Ajwain or Ajowain   Lovage

Aloo   Potato

Alu chole   A vegetarian dish using chickpeas, potatoes and tamarind

Alur dom   A dish using whole potatoes

Am   Mango

Am chur   Mango powder. A very sour flavouring agent

Anardana   Pomegranate

Aniseed   Saunf

Areca   Betel nut

Asafoetida   Hing. Gum obtained from root of giant fennel-like plant. Used in powder or resin form. A rather smelly spice

Aserio   Aniseed

Ata or Atta   Chupatti flour. Fine wholemeal flour used in most Indian breads. English wholemeal is a suitable alternative

B

Badain   Aniseed stars

Badam   Almond

Bargar   The process of frying whole spices in hot oil

Basmati   The best type of long-grain rice

Bay leaf   Tej Patia. This very well known leaf is used fresh or dried in certain Indian recipes

Besan   Chickpea flour

Bhajee or Bhaji   Dryish mild vegetable curry

Bhajia   Deep-fried fritter, usually onion. See Pakora

Bhare   Stuffed

Bharta or Bhurta   Mash or purée

Bhoona or Bhuna   The process of cooking the spice paste in hot oil. See Introduction. A bhoona curry is usually dry and cooked in coconut

Bhunana   Roast

Bindi   Okra

Biriani   A traditional dish. Rice baked with meat or vegetable filling

Black salt   Kala namak

Bombay Duck   A smallish fish native to the Bombay area known locally as Bommaloe Macchi. This was too hard for the British to pronounce so it became Bombay Duck. It is dried and appears on the table as a crispy deep fried starter or accompaniment to a curry

Bombay Potato   Small whole potatoes in curry and tomato sauce

Boti Kebab   Marinated cubes of lamb cooked in a tandoor oven

Brinjal   Aubergine

Burfi or Barfi   An Indian fudge-like sweetmeat made from reduced condensed milk in various flavours eg plain or pistachio (green)

C

Cardamom   Elaichi. Various types, notably green, white and brown. One of the most aromatic and expensive spices

Cashew nuts   Kaju

Cassia bark   A corky bark with a sweet fragrance similar to cinnamon. Cassia is coarser and cooks better than cinnamon and is used extensively in Northern Indian cookery. Although cooked in the curry the bark is too coarse to eat

Cayenne pepper   A type of chilli powder

Ceylon Curry   Usually cooked with coconut, lemon and chilli

Chaamp   Chop (eg lamb chop)

Chakla belan   Special rolling pin and board

Chamcha   Ladle

Chana   Type of lentil

Chawal   Rice

Chhalni   Sieve

Chilgoze or Nioze   Small long creamy nuts with brown shells used in cooking or eaten raw

Chilli   There are a great many species of chillies, which are the fleshy pods of shrub-like bushes of the capsicum family. Chillies range from large to small, and colours include green, white, purple, pink and red. Curiously, although synonymous with Indian food they were only brought to the sub-continent from South America some four centuries ago. They are now the most important heat agent in Indian cookery. They vary in hotness from mild to incendiary-like potency. Most commonly, small green or red chillies are used fresh. Red chillies can be dried and used whole, and chilli powder is made by grinding dried chillies.

Chimta   Tongs

Chirongi or Charauli   Small rounded nuts resembling Egyptian lentils. Used in puddings or pullaos.

Chor magaz   Melon seeds. Used as a thickener

Chupatti   A dry 6 inch (15 cm) disc of unleavened bread. Normally griddle cooked, it should be served piping hot. Spelling varies eg Chuppati, Chapati etc

Chutneys   The common ones are onion, mango and tandoori. There are dozens of others which rarely appear on the standard menu. (See Sambals.)

Cinnamon   Dalchini. The quill-like dried bark of the cinnamon tree. It is one of the most aromatic spices. Same family as cassia, it is generally used in dishes which require a delicate flavour

Cloves   Lavang

Coriander   Dhania. One of the most important spices in Indian cookery. The leaves of the plant can be used fresh and the seeds used whole or ground

Cummin or Cumin   Jeera. There are two types of seeds: white and black. The white seeds are a very important spice in Indian cookery. The black seeds (Kala Jeera) are seldom used. Both can be used whole or ground

Curry   The only word in this glossary to have no direct translation into any of the sub-continent's fifteen or so languages. The word was coined by the British in India centuries ago. Possible contenders for the origin of the word are, *Karahi* or *Karai* (Hindi), a wok-like frying pan used all over India to prepare masalas (spice mixtures); *Karhi* – a soup-like dish made with spices, chickpea flour dumplings and buttermilk; *Kari* – a spicy Tamil sauce; *Turkuri* – a seasoned sauce or stew; or *Kari Phulia*, neem or curry leaves (see below)

Curry leaves   Neem leaves or Kari Phulia. Small leaves a bit like bay leaves, used for flavouring

Cuscus   Poppy seed

D

Dahi   Yoghurt

Dahi wala   A meat dish cooked in a savoury yoghurt sauce

Dalchini or Darchim   Cinnamon

Degchi, Dekhchi or Degh   Brass or metal saucepan without handles also called Pateeli or Batloi

Dewa   Wooden spoon

Dhal   Lentils. There are over sixty types of lentil in the sub-continent. The common restaurant types are masoor (red which cooks yellow), chana and urid

Dhania   Coriander

Dhansak   Traditional chicken or meat dish cooked in lentil and vegetable purée

Dhungar   Applying the smoke of charcoal to ingredients

Do Piaza   Traditional meat dish. *Do* means two and *Piaza* means onion. It gets its name because onions appear twice in the cooking process

Doroo   Celery

Dosa or Dosai   A South Indian pancake made from rice and lentil flour. Usually served with a filling

Dum   Steam cooking. Long before the West invented the pressure cooker, India had her own method which lasts to this day. A pot with a close fitting lid is sealed with a ring of dough. The ingredients are then cooked in their own steam under some pressure

E

Ekuri   Spiced scrambled eggs

Elaichi   Cardamom

F

Fennel   Soonf

Fenugreek   Methi. This important spice is used as seeds and in fresh or dried leaf form. It is very savoury and is used in many Northern Indian dishes.

Foogath   Lightly cooked vegetable dish

G

Gajar   Carrot

Garam Masala   Literally 'hot mixture'. This refers to a blend of spices much loved in Northern Indian cookery. Curry Club Garam Masala contains nine spices (see Chapter 2)

Garlic   Lasan

Ghee   Clarified butter or margarine much used in Northern Indian cookery. The process is described in Chapter 2

Ginger   Adrak (fresh), Sont (dried); a rhizome which can be used fresh, dried or powdered. See Chapter 1

Gobi or Phoolgobi   Cauliflower

Goor or Gur   Jaggery (palm sugar) or molasses

Gosht   Lamb

Gram flour   Chickpea flour (Besan)

Gulab jaman   An Indian dessert. Small 1 inch (2.5 cm) diameter balls of flour and milk powder, deep-fried to golden and served cold in syrup. Cake-like texture

Gurda   Kidney. Gurda kebab is marinated kidney skewered and cooked in the tandoor

H

Halva   Sweets made from syrup and vegetables or fruit. Served cold in small squares. It is translucent and comes in bright colours depending on ingredient used; eg orange (carrot), green (pistachio), red (mango), etc. Has texture thicker than Turkish delight. Sometimes garnished with edible silver foil

Handi   Earthenware cooking pot

Hasina Kebab   Pieces of chicken breast, lamb or beef marinated in spices and then skewered and barbecued with onion, capsicum and tomato. Of Turkish origin

Hindi   Hindi is the official language of India. Although there are fourteen or so other languages in India, only Hindi translations have been used in this glossary. Spelling of Hindi words can vary in English because they are translated phonetically from many Hindi dialects

Hing   Asafoetida

Hisa   Bill (account)

Huldi   Turmeric

I

Idli   Rice and lentil flour cake served with light curry sauce. South Indian

Imli   Tamarind

Isgubul   Vegetable seed

J

Jaifal or Taifal   Nutmeg
Jal Frezi   Sauté or stir-fry
Jalebi   An Indian dessert. A flour, milk powder and yoghurt batter pushed through a narrow funnel into deep-frying oil to produce golden curly crispy rings. Served cold or hot in syrup
Javatri   Mace
Jeera or Zeera   Cummin
Jhanna   Flat slotted spoon
Jinga   Prawns

K

Kabli chana   Chickpeas
Kaddu kas   Grater
Kadhi   Yoghurt soup
Kaju   Cashew nut
Kala   Black
Kala jeera   Black cummin seeds
Kala namak   Black salt
Kaleji   Liver
Kalongi   Nigella, similar to wild onion seeds
Karahi   Karai, Korai etc. Cast iron, wok-like, frying or serving pan. See Curry
Karchhi   Metal flat 'spoon' used for turning frying ingredients
Karela   Small, dark green, knobbly vegetable of the gourd family
Kashmir chicken   Whole chicken stuffed with minced meat
Kashmir curry   Restaurateurs' creation. A sweetish curry often using lychees or similar ingredient
Kathal   Jack fruit
Katori   Small serving bowls which go on a thaali (tray)
Kebab   Skewered food cooked over charcoal. A process over 4000 years old which probably originated in the Middle East. It was imported to India by the Moslems centuries ago. (See Boti, Shami and Sheek Kebabs)
Keema   Minced meat curry
Kewra   Screwpine water. An extract of the flower of the tropical screwpine tree. It is a fragrant clear liquid used to flavour sweets. It is a cheap substitute for rosewater
Khalla musaria   Grinding stone or pounder
Khir   Technique of making a sort of cream. Milk is cooked with cucumber and puréed.
Khurzi   Lamb or chicken, whole with spicy stuffing
Kish mish   Sultanas
Kofta   Minced meat or vegetable balls in batter, deep-fried, and then cooked in a curry sauce
Kokum or Cocum   A variety of plum, pitted and dried. Prune-like and very sour. Also known in Malayan as Mangosteen
Korma   To most restaurants this just means a mild curry. Traditionally it is very rich. Meat, chicken or vegetables are cooked in cream, yoghurt and nuts, and are fragrantly spiced with saffron and aromatic spices
Koya   Reducing milk to a thick sticky solid. Used for sweet making
Kulcha   Small leavened bread
Kulcha, stuffed   Stuffed with mildly spiced mashed potato and baked in the tandoor
Kulfi   Indian ice cream. Traditionally it comes in vanilla, pistachio or mango flavours
Kus Kus   See Cuscus

L

Lasan   Garlic
Lhassi or Lassi   A refreshing drink made from yoghurt and crushed ice. The savoury version is Lhassi Namkeen and the sweet version is Lhassi Meethi
Lavang   Cloves
Lilva   A small oval-shaped bean which grows in a pod like the European pea
Loochees   A type of bread made in Bengal using white flour
Lovage   Ajwain or Ajowain

M

Macchi or Macchli   Fish

Mace   Javitri. The outer part of the nutmeg

Madras   You will not find a traditional recipe for Madras curry.... It is another restauratuers' invention. But the people of South India *do* eat hot curries; some original chef must have christened his hot curry 'Madras' and the name stuck

Makhani   A traditional dish. Tandoori chicken is cooked in a ghee and tomato sauce

Makke   Cornflour

Malai   Cream

Malaya   The curries of Malaya are traditionally cooked with plenty of coconut, chilli and ginger. In the Indian restaurant, however, they are usually mild and contain pineapple and other fruit

Mamra   Puffed Basmati rice

Masala   A mixture of spices which are cooked with a particular dish (see Chapter 1)

Masoor   Red lentil with green skin

Mathanni   Wooden whisk

Matka   Round earthenware pot used to freeze ice cream. It is filled with ice and salt.

Mattar   Green peas

Meethi   Sweet

Melon seeds   Chor magaz

Methi   Fenugreek

Mirch   Pepper or chilli

Moglai or Moghlai   Cooking in the style of the Moghul emperors whose chefs took Indian cookery to the heights of gourmet cuisine three centuries ago. Few restaurateurs who offer Moglai dishes come anywhere near this excellence. True Moglai dishes are expensive and time-consuming to prepare authentically

Mollee   Fish dishes cooked in coconut and chilli

Mooli   Large white radish

Moong   One of the more commonly used lentils. It has a green skin and can be used whole, split or polished to make various dhals

Mulligatawny   A Tamil sauce (*Molegoo* – pepper, *Tunny* – water) which has become well known as a British soup

Munacca   Raisins

Murgh   Chicken

Murgh Masala(m)   A speciality dish of whole chicken, marinated in yoghurt and spices for 24 hours then stuffed and roasted

N

Namak   Salt

Namkeen   Salty

Nan or Naan   Leavened bread baked in the tandoor. It is teardrop shaped and about 8–10 inches long (20–25 cm). It must be served fresh and hot

Nan Keema   Nan bread stuffed with a thin layer of minced meat curry then baked in the tandoor.

Nan Peshwari   Nan bread stuffed with almonds and/or cashew and/or raisins and baked in the tandoor

Nargis Kebab   Indian scotch egg – spiced minced meat around a hard-boiled egg

Naryal   Coconut

Neem   Curry leaf (see Curry)

Nigella   See Kalonji

Nimboo   Lime (lemon)

Nutmeg   Jaifal

O

Okra   Bindi. A pulpy vegetable also known as ladies' fingers

P

Pan or Paan   Betel leaf folded around a stuffing – lime paste or various spices (see Supari) and eaten after a meal as a digestive

Pakoras   To all intents and purposes the same as the Bhajia

Palak or Sag   Spinach

Panch Phoran   Five seeds. A mixture of five spices used in Bengali vegetable cooking, comprising equal amounts of cummin, fennel, fenugreek, mustard and wild onion seeds

Paneer   Cheese made from bottled milk which can be fried and curried (Mattar Paneer)

Papadam   Thin lentil flour wafers. When cooked (deep fried or baked) they expand to about 8 inches (20 cm). They must be crackling crisp and warm when served. If not send them back to be re-heated and deduct points from that restaurant. They come plain or spiced with lentils, pepper, garlic or chilli. (See Chapter 1)

Paprika   Mild red pepper made from capsicums. It originally came from Hungary and only reached India this century. Its main use is to give red colour to a dish

Paratha   A deep-fried bread

Pasanda   Meat, usually lamb, beaten and cooked in one piece

Patia   Restaurant seafood curry with thick, dark brown, sweet and sour sauce

Patna   A long-grained rice

Pepper   Mirch. Has for centuries been India's most important spice, gaining it the title 'king of spices'. It grows on vines which flower triennially and produce clusters of berries, which are picked and dried and become the peppercorns. Green, black and white pepper are not different varieties. All peppercorns are green when picked and must be bottled or freeze-dried at once to retain the colour. Black pepper is the dried berry. White pepper is obtained by soaking off the black skin of the berry. Peppercorns are a heat agent and can be used whole or gound

Phal or Phall   A very hot curry (the hottest) invented by restaurateurs

Piaz, Peeaz or Pyaz   Onion

Pickles   Pungent, hot pickled vegetables or meat essential to an Indian meal. Most common are Lime, Mango and Chilli

Pistachio nut   Pista magaz. A fleshy, tasty nut which can be used fresh (the greener the better) or salted. It is expensive and goes well in savoury or sweet dishes such as Biriani or Pista Kulfi (ice cream)

Podina   Mint leaves or powder

Poha   Pounded rice

Prawn butterfly   Jinga Praj Patia. Prawn marinated in spices and fried in batter

Prawn Puri   Prawns in a hot sauce served on puri bread

Pullao   Rice and meat or vegetables cooked together in a pan until tender. In many restaurants the ingredients are mixed after cooking to save time (see also Biriani)

Pullao Rice   The restaurant name for rice fried with spices and coloured yellow

Pulses   Types of lentils

Puri   A deep fried unleavened bread about 4 inches (10 cm) in diameter. It puffs up when cooked and should be served at once

Q

Quas Chawal or Kesar Chaval
Rice fried in ghee, flavoured and coloured with saffron

R

Rai   Mustard seed

Raita   A cooling chutney of yoghurt and vegetable, cucumber for instance, which accompanies the main meal

Rajma   Red kidney beans

Rasgulla   Walnut-sized balls of semolina and cream cheese cooked in syrup (literal meaning 'juicy balls'). They are white or pale gold in colour and served cold or warm

Rashmi Kebab   Kebab minced meat inside a net-like omelette casing

Rasmalai Rasgullas cooked in cream and served cold. A very rich sweet

Rhogan Josh Gosht Literally means 'red juice lamb'. It can be spelt dozens of ways. It is a traditional Northern Indian dish. Lamb is marinated in yoghurt then cooked with ghee and spices and tomato. It should be creamy and spicy but not too hot

Ratin jot Alkanet root. Beetroot coloured, dried, wafer-thin bark of the root. It is used as a deep red dye for make-up, clothing and food. Traditionally the Northerners obtained their red Tandoori and Rhogan Josh Gosht colouring from it

Rosewater Ruh gulab. A clear essence extracted from rose petals to give fragrance to sweets. See Kewra

Roti Bread

Ruh gulab Rosewater essence

S

Sabzi A generic term for vegetables

Saffron Kesar or Zafron. The world's most expensive spice, saffron is the stamen of the crocus flower. It takes 70,000 stamens to make 100 g (about 3½ oz). A few stamens are all that are needed to give a recipe a delicate yellow colouring and aroma

Sag or Saag Spinach

Salt Namak

Sambals A Malayan term describing the side dishes accompanying the meal. Sometimes referred to on the Indian menu

Sambar A South Indian vegetable curry made largely from lentils

Samosa The celebrated triangular deep fried meat or vegetable patties served as starters or snacks

Sarson Ka Sag Mustard leaves (spinach-like)

Saunf or Souf Aniseed

Seeng Drumstick. A bean-like variety of marrow which looks exactly like a drumstick

Seenl Allspice. Related to the clove family, the seed resembles small dried peas. Called allspice because its aroma seems to combine those of clove, cinnamon, ginger, nutmeg and pepper. Used rather more in European cooking than Indian

Sesame Til

Shami Kebab Round minced meat rissoles

Shashlik Cubes of skewered lamb

Sheek or Seekh Kebab Spiced minced meat shaped on a skewer and grilled or barbecued

Sil batta A pair of grinding stones: *Sil*, large stone, *Batta*, small pounder

Sonf Fennel seed

Sont or Sonth Dry ginger

Sorportel A Goan pork dish with heart, liver and meat

Sub-continent Term to describe India, Pakistan, Bangladesh, Nepal, Burma, and Sri Lanka as a group

Supari Mixture of seeds and sweeteners for chewing after a meal. Usually includes aniseed or fennel, shredded betel nut, sugar balls, marrow seeds etc

T

Taipal or Jaiphal Nutmeg

Tamarind Imli. A date-like fruit used as a chutney, and in cooking as a souring agent (see Chapter 1)

Tandoori A style of charcoal cooking originating in North-West India (what is now Pakistan and the Punjab). Originally it was confined to chicken and lamb (see Boti Kebab) and Nan bread. More recently it is applied to lobster etc. The meat is marinated in a reddened yoghurt sauce and placed in the tandoor (clay oven)

Taraazu Weighing scales

Tarbooj ke beej Watermelon seeds

Tarka Garnish of spices/onion

Tarka dhal Lentils fried and garnished with spices

Tava or Tawa Heavy steel shallow frying pan

Tej Patia Bay leaf

Thaali A tray which holds the complete meal served in individual bowls (Katori). Used by diners in the South

Tikka Skewered meat, chicken or seafood, marinated then barbecued or tandoori baked

Til Sesame seed

Tinda A vegetable of the cucumber family

Tindaloo See Vindaloo

Toor or Toovar Type of lentil

Tukmeria or Tulsi Black seeds of a basil family plant. Look like poppy seeds. Used in drinks

Turmeric Haldi or Huldi. A very important Indian spice, turmeric is a rhizome. The fresh root is used occasionally as a vegetable or in pickles. The ground spice is extensively used to give the familiar yellow colour to curries. Use sparingly or it can cause bitterness

Tusci Basil

U

Udrak Ginger

Urid A type of lentil. Its husk is black and it comes whole, split or polished. Available as a dhal dish in some restaurants

V

Vanaspati Starch

Vark or Varak Edible silver or gold foil

Vindaloo A fiery hot dish from Goa. Traditionally it was pork marinated in vinegar with potato (Aloo). In the restaurant it has now come to mean just a very hot dish. Also sometimes called Bindaloo or Tindaloo (even hotter)

X

Xacutti A Goan dish using chicken and coconut

Y

Yakni Mutton

Z

Zafron Saffron

Zeera Cummin

INDEX